RADICAL
REFLECTION

RADICAL
REFLECTION
and the Origin of the
Human Sciences

by
Calvin O. Schrag

Purdue University Press
West Lafayette, Indiana
1980

Library of Congress Catalog Card Number 79-91085
International Standard Book Numbers
clothbound edition, 0-911198-57-1
paperbound edition, 0-911198-58-X
Printed in the United States of America

To my wife and my daughter
Virginia Marie and Heather Sue

CONTENTS

PREFACE

This is a book about the human sciences. It is not, however, a treatise on scientific methodology nor is it a proposal for a unification of the human sciences through an integration of their findings within a general conceptual scheme. The underlying question that directs the inquiry points us to a different region. It is the question of the *possibility* of the human sciences, and throughout the book this question takes the form of a quest for their origins. The proximate circumstance that impels this quest is the evident crisis in the current sciences of man. The human sciences comprise a tottering Tower of Babel in which each speaks with its own tongue, producing a virtual breakdown of communication not only among the several human sciences themselves but also within the republic of human knowledge more generally. Their accelerated development within recent years has produced such a proliferation of portraits and models of man that the common center from which they allegedly proceed is no longer recognizable. There is indeed some justifiable concern as to whether the several human sciences are any longer interested in asking the question about man's understanding of himself and his world. In our quest for the origin, we want to reclaim and revitalize this question. This question, which would seem to provide the initial motivation for any human science, appears to be forgotten during the investigator's trek to his laboratory and his persistent preoccupation with methodological matters. The human sciences are suffering from a loss of center, from an occlusion of that point of origin at which man first asks the question about himself. Can this common center be restored through a disciplined search for that origin from which the human sciences themselves proceed? This is the underlying concern and the pivotal question of the present work.

This book is also, and at the same time, a book about the philosophical study of man. This is unavoidably the case, and not simply because the book is written by a philosopher but because the question that is asked relative to the origin of the human sciences must also be put to the community of philosophers whose business it is to reflect on the nature of man. Here too we find a crisis of conceptualization taking place. The philosophical literature on the being and behavior of man is a veritable labyrinth of concepts—mind, consciousness, ego, self, subject, essence, existence, action, structure, praxis, and many more—all designed to deliver knowledge of man. Yet these concepts often work at cross-purposes and seem in the end only to lead us farther and farther from the phenomenon under investigation.

The format that we have devised for interrogating the issue of origin as it pertains to the scientific and philosophical study of man begins appropriately with a critique of philosophical anthropology. It is this relatively recent discipline that has been entrusted with the task of coming to terms with the existing crisis in the study of man. Although sharing the concern of philosophical anthropology about the loss of center in the various sciences and philosophies of man, we have been compelled to initiate a critique of the presuppositions of the project of philosophical anthropology itself. We are critical of the continuation of an idealistically oriented philosophy of consciousness within the presuppositional framework of philosophical anthropology. Philosophical anthropology has been inclined to formulate the question about man as an inquiry into a possible subject of consciousness. This subject of consciousness in turn has had its status defined through the instrumentation of a transcendental-empirical dichotomy. One of the tasks that we have set for radical reflection is that of overcoming this dichotomy. Our critique also brings under scrutiny the effort on the part of philosophical anthropology to rectify the current crisis in the human sciences by coordinating and integrating the various disciplines through an appeal to philosophical foundations. The path of our inquiry leads us beyond the metaphor of foundations as it is utilized in philosophical reflection. This follows from our requirement for a radical reflection that is able to penetrate to the prephilosophical and prescientific origin of self-understanding and world-comprehension. Radical reflection approaches the task at issue not as one of integrating the several sciences and philosophies of man through a sublation of their results into a unifying conceptual scheme, but rather as an inquiry into that originary setting of world experience that antedates both scientific explanation and philosophical construction.

Radical reflection, as we illustrate it, thus simultaneously critiques the human sciences and philosophical anthropology. The path of this reflection leads to a radicalization of knowledge, to a radicalization of value, and then to a hermeneutic of everyday life that exhibits a new posture of understanding and an expanded notion of reason. The radicalization of knowlege makes possible a deconstruction of the transcendental-empirical doublet, and the radicalization of value is geared toward a dismantling of the fact-value dichotomy. This radicalization of knowledge and value requires a new hermeneutic that transfigures the traditional philosophical concepts of understanding and reason by reinserting them into the concrete texture of meaning-formation in everyday life. Thus any scientific and philosophical study of man is confronted with the challenge of establishing a reflexivity upon the originary matrix of thought, language, and action, from which scientific and philosophical constructs arise.

In the concluding chapter, it is shown how this return to the origin demands an expanded notion of reason, which not only marks out the possibility of technical reason in scientific and philosophical thought but also encompasses the constellations of mytho-poetic signification. This expanded notion of reason includes the *logos* of *mythos* that resides in the concrete multivalence of significations informing the body of mythology. In this reclamation of the origin, we discern neither a denial of scientific explanation nor an elimination of philosophical analysis, but rather a realignment of the projects of a science and a philosophy of man so as to make them reflexive upon the actual context and ongoing stream of precategorial world experience.

The above comprises the central thesis and thrust of the present work. Throughout our probings and explorations we have made an effort to remain cognizant of the contributions to the general issue which have been made by some of the representatives of phenomenology, structuralism, critical theory, and linguistic philosophy. At crucial points we have been compelled to contest the formulations and conclusions of some of the representatives of these current modes of philosophizing. This, however, has been done not to stage academic debates but rather to further clarify and understand the basic issues through critical dialogue. When an author finds the position or argument of an opponent worthy of criticism, it is an indication that he has already learned a great deal from him.

After having completed a work such as this, the author is quite naturally inclined to acknowledge various individuals whose advice and criticism helped minimize the shortcomings of the finished project. At the same time, he is aware of the risks in such an acknowledgement, knowing how easy it is to overlook some persons whose contributions have made their presence felt throughout the pages. We shall, however, assume this risk and acknowledge the following individuals who have read the manuscript either in part or in its entirety and have offered the benefit of their wisdom on many points. My colleagues in the Department of Philosophy at Purdue, Richard F. Grabau, Jeffrey Maitland, and William L. McBride, have participated with me in a continuing Socratic dialogue pertinent to the issues discussed in the manuscript. Prof. Fred R. Dallmayr, Dee Professor of Political Science at the University of Notre Dame and Prof. Hwa Yol Jung of the Department of Political Science at Moravian College also read the manuscript in various stages of its development and forced me to address somewhat more specifically the current issues in social and political theory. Prof. Lawrence Grossberg of the Department of Speech Communication at the University of Illinois provided helpful criticism from the perspective of another related human science. Prof. Karl Otto-Apel of Frankfurt University and Prof. Wolf Mays of the University of Manchester, during their tenures as visiting professors at Purdue, supplied constant stimulation and insight during our periodic discussions on the interface of philosophy and the human sciences. I wish also to acknowledge the twelve participants in my 1978 National Endowment for the Humanities summer seminar for college teachers, dealing with the topic of "Philosophical Anthropology in Contemporary European Thought," for their enthusiastic response to the central thesis of this work and their encouragement to make it available in published form. To all of the above individuals I offer my very special thanks. As they peruse the published manuscript, I am confident that they will find that their recommendations and critical suggestions did indeed make a difference. In conclusion I wish to acknowledge the American Council of Learned Societies and express my appreciation for a generous grant-in-aid without which the completion and publication of this book would unquestionably have been delayed.

CHAPTER 1

The Current Crisis in the Human Sciences

There is today a widespread awareness that a crisis in the human sciences has taken place. Philosophers and social scientists alike have expressed increasing concern about this apparent lapse of the sciences of man into a situation of crisis. Regrettably, however, no clear and consistent account of the nature of this crisis and the factors that have occasioned it has been forthcoming. Indeed, the varied and conflicting accounts of the nature and source of the enroaching crisis have become infected with a conceptual crisis of their own.

The definition of the problem at issue is complicated by the fact that within the general situation of crisis that pervades the human sciences there are crises which are indigenous to the special disciplines of psychology, sociology, anthropology, political science, and history.[1] Various species of psychologism, sociologism, and historicism at the same time threaten the validation of intramural truth claims within these disciplines and obstruct any unification and integration of the special human sciences as common contributors toward a scientific knowledge of man. Psychologism within psychology cannot avoid the application of reductive principles to itself, whereby the conceptualization within its own discipline becomes simply another expression of psychological intentions, resulting in the displacement of any stable criteria of validation. Sociologism within sociology leads to the abandonment of all contents of culture, as well as the thought processes of the sociologist himself, to the variations of a changing social milieu, which then sacrifices the truth of its own position and precludes any possibility of communication with the other human sciences. Similarly, historicism within history sacrifices itself on the altar of its own experiment and culminates in a relativization of the present, in which neither conceptual nor normative claims can have an obliging character.

The consciousness of crisis within the special sciences of man

1

becomes intensified with the awareness of a proliferation of various images and models that has resulted from the constructionist procedures within the recent history of the several human sciences. The image of man as *"homo oeconomicus"* has been in the literature for some time, but more recently we have become heirs to a colorful variety of new portraits. These include *"homo politicus"* (Lasswell); *"homo sociologicus"* (Dahrendorf); *"homo symbolicus"* (Cassirer); *"homo ludens"* (Huizinga); *"homo viator"* (Marcel); *"homo significans"* (Barthes); "psychological man" (Rieff); and "ecclesial man" (Farley).[2] Add to this list some of the classical images of man that have intermittently appeared in Western philosophy and literature—such as *homo religiosus, homo sapiens, homo faber, homo dionysiacus,* and *homo creator*—and it becomes evident even to the casual observer that we are saddled with a veritable crisis of concepts in the scientific and philosophical study of man. Admittedly, we are assured by at least one of the more recent architects of scientific images of man that the image is only a "scientific construct" and "not primarily a description of reality."[3] Yet, this does little to attentuate the conceptual crisis that the proliferations of such scientific constructs occasion. Furthermore, in spite of the repeated assurances that one is dealing here with methodological devices rather than statements about what is the case, some ground still remains for critical concern. Scientific constructs, as part of the methodological edifice, have a way of taking on the more durable armor of ontological claims.

This conceptual crisis brought about by the proliferation of images and models of man in the various disciplines was already eloquently articulated by Max Scheler in his 1928 essay, *Man's Place in Nature*. In this work Scheler writes: "Man is more a problem to himself at the present time than ever before in all recorded history. . . . We have a scientific, a philosophical, and a theological anthropology in complete separation from each other. We do not have a unified idea of man. The increasing multiplicity of the special sciences, valuable as they are, tends to hide man's nature more than reveal it."[4] Ernst Cassirer, two decades later, provided a remarkably similar assessment of the current situation within the human sciences. "Psychology, ethnology, anthropology, and history have amassed an astoundingly rich and constantly increasing body of facts. . . . But our wealth of facts is not necessarily a wealth of thoughts. Unless we succeed in finding a clue of Ariadne to lead us out of this labyrinth, we can have no real insight into the general character of human culture; we shall remain lost in a mass of disconnected and disintegrated data which seem to lack all conceptual unity."[5]

In more recent times, Georges Gusdorf has voiced his concern over the distressing state of affairs in the human sciences: "We need only to consider the present state of the human sciences to ascertain that they are in complete confusion. They are developing, most certainly, and they are multiplying their works, but the technicians of the various disciplines usually do not know precisely what they want nor what they are doing."[6] This sentiment is reflected by Gusdorf's fellow countryman Paul Ricoeur when he says: "The sciences of man are dispersed into separate disciplines and literally do not know what they are talking about."[7] Scheler, Cassirer, Gusdorf, and Ricoeur are not alone in their testimonies to the widespread crisis that permeates the developing sciences of man. Not only professional philosophers and scientists but also the popular press intermittently recognize the conceptual disarray and lack of sense of direction that has settled in on academe in its pursuit of knowledge of man and society. This general testimony, along with specific assessments such as those of Scheler, Cassirer, Gusdorf, and Ricoeur, provides our point of departure for an analysis and elucidation of the nature and source of the current crisis in the contemporary sciences of man.

We will begin by examining some candidates for explanation which have achieved some currency in the literature but which upon careful scrutiny need to be disqualified. We need to proceed with some caution in attempting to locate the source of the crisis because of the persisting proclivity to mistake symptoms for causes. Explanations for the crisis in the human sciences abound both in the philosophical and scientific literature, but many of these explanations do not proceed beyond the surface manifestations of the phenomenon. The increasingly popular indictment of the specialization which characterizes the developing human sciences is a case in point. Some profess to have found the source of the crisis in specialization, contending that the very division of labor whereby sociology is separated from psychology, anthropology from political science, and all of these from history is the original sin from which all manner of tragic consequences follow. Admittedly, much *excessive* specialization passes before our eyes in academe; and often we suspect this to be a cloak designed to hide the presuppositions of a particular discipline so as to protect them from critical attacks from the outside. Needless to say, interdisciplinary communication and the unified pursuit of knowledge of man cannot thrive within such a milieu. Yet, it is surely a mistake to single out specialization itself, the division of the human sciences into distinguishable areas of inquiry, as the cause of the crisis. Indeed, the division of intellectual labor in the scientific study of man would seem to be necessitated by the finite character of human knowledge. We can approach the complex phenomena of man and society only perspectively, and the several human sciences provide such several human perspectives. Specialization as an implication of finitude is not in itself a mark of crisis. Only when specialization *goes wrong* do we have a crisis situation. And what it is that has gone wrong is not yet accounted for.

Another frequently expressed diagnosis of the source of the crisis finds the cause in the increasing preoccupation with quantification and formalization. There seems to be something unsettling about the theory and practice of measurement, about the elaborate statistical models, that are so much a part of contemporary research in the human sciences. Sometimes, and particularly for those whose interests or talents do not reside with matters mathematical, it is merely a feeling of distrust about something outside the range of their interests or competencies. Or it may be a general puzzlement of how numbers can have anything to do with people. At other times, however, this distrust and puzzlement become intensified and congeal into a veritable *Kulturangst* in which theories of measurement and statistics are singled out as wicked devices in the hands of wicked men who are waiting for the opportune moment to depersonalize everything that still has a residue of humanity. This broadside indictment of the use of quantification and formalization in the human sciences, levied from time to time in the counter-culture literature and the literature of popular existentialism, may in the end be not only premature but also wide of the mark. Clarity on the issue at hand requires a distinction between a justifiable use of quantification and formalization and their distortion under the conditions of misapplication.

As part of the methodological design of any given research project in the human sciences, the use of quantification and formalization is in itself quite harmless and undisturbing. We find nothing wrong in principle with counting and measuring. In calibrating the responses of a psychological subject, in using sociometric techniques for determining voting patterns within a certain precinct, in predicting the ups and downs of the gross national product, there is an unavoidable and legitimate need for the use of quantification procedures. Such a use of quantification has been with us for some time. Marx had already designed a questionnaire, and even a century earlier various types of measuring procedures were used in the study of society. Although currently somewhat in vogue in the human sciences, measurement, quantification, and formalization have a history that extends back into the nineteenth and eighteenth centuries; and it is difficult, at least on first reading, to find any intrinsic fault with the use of such procedures. Even more prejudgmental would it be to say that the use of measurement, quantification, and formalization are the corporate cause of the crisis in the current sciences of man.

These frequent attacks on the proliferating use of quantification procedures do, however, provide an oblique reference to the crisis of the human sciences. An articulation of some of its symptoms indicates the source of the crisis. Two such symptoms are often discernible whenever we see an excessive preoccupation with measurement and statistical analysis. We shall name these symptoms "methodological naïveté" and "methodological pretension," respectively. Methodological naïveté, in its simplest form, is the slippage of elementary logic in assuming more universality in the results of statistical study than the sampling and measuring afford. But a more subtle and more distressing ingredient is often found operative in what we here call methodological naïveté. This has to do with the arrogation of a certain epistemic privilege to quantitatively directed inquiry, which often takes on a quasi-religious coloring, achieving its sanction through the commandment, "Thou shalt be empirical!" But it is precisely at this point that the naïveté comes to the surface, for the commandment carries with it all sorts of unspoken presuppositions as to what counts as empirical. Already at work here is the easy and unwarranted assumption that the methods of measurement and quantification are *more* empirical than are other methods. In the end the empirical is identified with the quantitatively measurable. This unwarranted privilege of a *mathesis* of the quantifiable has itself come under attack by certain social scientists who seem to have a broader understanding and more acute sense of the range and reach of the empirical. A case in point is the research and analysis designed by Harold Garfinkel. Garfinkel's *ethnomethodology,* in which the rational properties of indexical expressions embedded in the concrete and ordinary features of communication become the subject of analysis, provides a sheet-anchor against any absolutization of quantification procedures.[8]

The other symptom discernible in this area which points to a crisis in the sciences of man is methodological pretension. Here we are dealing with a tendency, usually tacit and surreptitious, to incorporate reality claims into the methodological procedures themselves. In the movement of methodological pretension, the method determines the content, the theory predefines the reality under investigation, and the tail wags the proverbial dog. This follows in the wake of methodological naïveté which confers upon the method of quantification an epistemic privilege and defines it as *the* way to empirical reality. But in the moment this is done, the experiential is pretentiously reduced to the experimental; and reality is prejudged as statistical or measurable "fact." However, the question of the meaning of fact, to say nothing about the meaning of reality (social or otherwise), is not a question that can be answered by a species of methodological fiat. Nor should the unspoken assumption as to the priority of method over content remain unexamined. The role and function of methodology itself need to be addressed through critical reflection. The presuppositions relative to the use of a particular methodology, the meaning of fact, and the insinuation of reality claims should be brought under scrutiny.

Thus the possibility, and perhaps distressing prevalence, of methodological naïveté and methodological pretension needs to be referenced as a symptom of a crisis which itself may well lie on the hither side of the issue of scientific methodology per se. But the point ought to be reiterated that these methodological aberrations are no indictment of the use of measurement, quantification, and formalization in themselves. The crisis in the human sciences does not reside in the research hardware that social scientists from time to time are disposed to employ. The genuine source of the crisis will need to be found elsewhere.

Within the current literature on the subject, we find another common candidate for the explanation of the crisis. This is technology; and since its candidacy has been announced, a great deal of ink has been consumed and much passion expressed in debates on "technology vs. antitechnology." In the end what is at issue in such debates is the problem of value—a problem which, of course, has been with us for some time. This problem is usually posed in the most general terms, articulated as the problem of the threat of technology to the human values that buttress civilization—past, present, and future. This opens the debate to a rather colorful variety of affirmers and negators, including natural scientists, social scientists, philosophers, theologians, historians, literary critics, and even the anonymous "man on the street." Certainly everyone must have a voice in such a pervasive and all-encompassing issue! Yet, upon reflection, there seems to be something hollow about these current, impassioned debates on technology and value, not only because the issues are defined with such distressing vagueness but also because of the unspoken presuppositions about value on which the debate seems to rest. What usually remains unrecognized is that the issues in the debate reduce to a matter of competing moralities, without attentiveness to or even awareness of the inquiry-standpoint from which these moralities emerge. The basic question as to the origin of value remains unasked.

In moving from the very general statement of the threat-of-technology theme, vis-à-vis the effect of technology on the quality of human life, to the more specific expression of this alleged threat in the designs and investigations of the special sciences of man, it becomes possible to localize the issue with somewhat more precision. Some critics of technology claim that the human sciences themselves have become technologized with respect to both their procedures and goals and that this accounts for the current crisis in the science of man. Such technologization, it is alleged, can be seen at work, for example, in B. F. Skinner's project of developing a "technology of human behavior."[9] The fashion today, both within the circles of the learned and the circles of the vulgar, is to use Skinner's neobehaviorism as a likely target for an antitechnology critique. This may well be due to the fact that Skinner's Achilles' heel is so vulnerable. His technology of human behavior is layered with numerous unspoken value-presuppositions regarding what is good, what counts as culture, and why it should survive. But what the antitechnologists offer as a counter-proposal does not proceed beyond an appeal to a competing system of moral values.

The issue, we suggest, is at bottom a somewhat more complex one than that of the technological implications of the methods and goal of science. It becomes at the same time an issue of the *origin* of science and the *origin* of value. At most the technology vs. value debate is a symptom of a more fundamental estranged state of affairs. Now to reformulate the issue in a more methodologically conscious manner as an issue of fact vs. value is of little help here, for this issue too is symptomatic of a conceptual crisis on a deeper level. The fact-value distinction, which has played such a large role in the current controversies on the nature and goal of the human sciences, is itself a reified result of the confrontation of an abstracted empiricism with an objectified system of value. What is thus required is an interrogation of the originative senses of fact and value as they emerge within the fabric of human affairs. We need to reask the Nietzschean questions regarding the "genealogy of morals" and "the transvaluation of value," and supplement these questions with an interrogation of the genealogy of *technē* and the possible transfiguration of the meaning of fact. Only then will the presuppositions of abstracted empricism and the problematic character of the language of value-theory be brought to light, making it possible for us to deal with genuine causes rather than symptoms in addressing the question of the crisis in the sciences of man. It will thus be necessary for us to devote a subsequent chapter to a deconstruction of the fact-value problematic (Chapter 4: "The World of Fact and Value").

Thus far we have examined three possible candidates which might serve as explanations for the current crisis in the human sciences: specialization, quantification and formalization, and the increasing impact of technology on scientific investigation particularly and on human life more generally. We have found these proposed explanations, for the most part, bereft of genuine explanatory force. Neither specialization nor quantification and formalization nor technology, in and of themselves, seems to possess crisis-making qualities. To identify a crisis, a more fundamental disproportion needs to be articulated; and this is not achieved by the critics of culture who inveigh against the division of labor in scientific investigation, the use of quantifying techniques, and the threats of technology. Admittedly, there may be a tacit recognition by these critics that what has gone awry is a misuse, overextension, or absolutization of certain methodological principles and procedures. But even this, we suggest, is but a recognition of the symptoms of the crisis and not yet a specification of its source.

Now there are those — possibly of a more philosophical persuasion — who will be prone to look for a somewhat broader perspective to explain the crisis. Might it not be urged that the crisis in the sciences of man has its source in the proliferation of the various "philosophies" that have settled in on the contemporary scene and insinuated themselves in various ways into the methodological designs and goals of the special human sciences? Continuing in this vein, might we then not argue that the resolution to the crisis consists in locating or fashioning that "true" philosophy which will provide a secure and stable foundation and supply the sciences of man with a direction and principle of unification? Could it be that the crisis is the result of competing philosophies — positivism, existentialism, phenomenology, Marxism, structuralism, linguistic analysis — all vying for ascendency and providing the sciences of man with conflicting directives?

However alluring such a line of inquiry might be — particularly for professional philosophers — it will again be our contention that knowledge of the source of the crisis is not established thus, nor is the suggested path for the resolution of the crisis a viable one. Again, at best, the phenomenon of conflicting philosophical bases for the human sciences, and the volatile methodological controversies that have become part of this phenomenon (such as the celebrated *Methodenstreit* of the early sixties, which pitted the positivists against the Marxists) are themselves symptoms of a deeper disturbance in man's project of achieving knowledge of himself. The various competing philosophies, and philosophy itself as a discipline, are themselves inseparably a part of the crisis. There is a crisis within philosophical analysis and construction that inevitably attaches to the crisis in the sciences of man. Philosophical reason itself has gravitated into a situation of crisis, and it will no longer do to appeal to such philosophical reason to provide the unimpeachable foundation and unifying principle for the various researches into the nature and behavior of man. What is required, in short, for a genuine assessment of the source of the crisis and a pointing of the way to its possible resolution is a move to a more radical form of reflection, a *protophilosophical* and *protoscientific* reflection that antedates the conceptualization and typification that is at work in the formalizations of philosophy and science.

The path of this radical reflection, we submit, will lead to a comprehension of the current crisis as a loss of an originative questioning in man's search for self knowledge. The human sciences and philosophy alike have failed to come to terms with the rigorous and multifaceted questioning implied in the Socratic injunction, "Know Thyself." The sense and urgency of this questioning has been suppressed. In the scientific and philosophical literature, we are bombarded with a plethora of images, myths, and models of man, embedded within a conceptual labyrinth, which leads us from one artificial construct to another, until like Theseus himself we lose our way and are cut off from the point of entry. Our crisis becomes a crisis of concepts, of methodologies, of universal philosophies that have lost their way because their point of *origin* has been occluded. The originative question, and the situation of questioning in which the originative question was posed, is lost in an entangling network of concepts and constructs. Man can no longer ask the question about himself and consequently fails to grasp his situation of crisis as residing in a crisis of self-understanding, because the primordial motivation of the questioning has been forgotten. It is this *loss of origin* on the part of both scientific investigation and philosophical analysis that occasions the current event of crisis. The implicatory requirement for any philosophy and science of man is thus the establishment of a reflexivity whereby the originative questioning of man about himself, within a precategorial and prescientific matrix of human experience, is recovered.

Consequently, the inquiry into the contributing factors that have produced the current crisis in the varied sciences and philosophies of man is inseparable from the question of origin, for we will be able to understand the crisis only when we perceive how it is that science and philosophy alike have been uprooted from their origin. Clearly such an approach and projected goal seem to place a considerable weight on the notion of origin; and the reader will justifiably demand, even at this early stage of investigation, an initial clarification of the sense of origin at issue in the proposed central thesis. Some of the initial clarification will need to take the form of a promissory note, which hopefully will be redeemed by the time that the reader finishes the last chapter. The thematic of origin is the undergirding thematic of the entire work, and its' elucidation requires the sustained analysis of the succeeding chapters. Nonetheless, some initial clarification of what is at stake in the question of origin must be provided at this juncture.

The word "origin" has become heir to a number of different meanings. Probably the most common meaning is that of temporal beginning, which might within varying contexts refer to a scientific-cosmological beginning (origin of the universe), or a biological beginning (the origin of life), or the beginning of a cultural movement or institution (the origin of the modern nation-state). Now it should already be evident that when we speak of the "origin of the human sciences" it is not this sense of origin that is at issue. Admittedly, there is an external, sequential history in which the human sciences have developed. We can with some intelligibility speak of the origin of sociology in the thought and investigations of Auguste Comte. We can speak of the development of psychology from Aristotle to Freud. We can speak of the rise and development of political economy. Within such a context the meaning of origin is chronologically and historiographically understood. This sense of origin is legitimate in its own right, but it is not the sense of origin with which we are concerned in this study.

There is another sense of origin that can be justified, particularly in philosophical writings. This is the meaning of origin as metaphysical first principle, which has played such an important role in the history of Western philosophy. This sense of origin appears intermittently throughout the history of thought in the guise of "first cause," "infinite substance," or "primordial cosmic force." It has been the destiny of this sense of origin to be aligned with theological considerations, thus defining it within a theo-metaphysical scheme of inquiry. From this perspective, the question of origin is a theo-metaphysical posturing of the pre-Socratic question concerning the *archē*. As is well known, in the development of post-Socratic metaphysical thought in the West this meaning of origin traveled with the use of a categorical scheme (principally substance and causality) designed to explain the source and status of metaphysical entities, both real and ideal.[10] Again, we wish to propose a suspension of this notion in the hope of disclosing a sense of origin which is more *originative* vis-à-vis the question of the philosophy and sciences of man.

A modification of the classical metaphysical notion of origin has taken place in the development of modern thought, occasioned by the influences of British empiricism on the one hand and Kant's critical philosophy on the other. Origin is here understood epistemologically, as a prior set of conditions, either the conditions of psychological acts (Hume and Mill) or the prior logical conditions of categorical operation (Kant). Recognizing certain variations which occurred from time to time, this circumscribes the approach to the meaning of origin in modern empiricism and rationalism, proceeding principally within the context of epistemological concerns. The question of origin is pursued within a framework of cognitive interests geared to the establishment of a valid theory of knowledge. This modern *epistēmē,* in which empiricist and rationalist at times go their separate ways and at times join forces in the interests of common philosophical cause, has conferred an indelible character on all contemporary thought, philosophical as well as scientific. We are conditioned to think epistemologically. And to think epistemologically is to think logically and methodologically. Yet, as we think, and unavoidably so, within this sedimented epistemic framework, we wish to propose the performance of a radical *epochē,* a suspension of beliefs and presuppositions, to enable us to get a glimpse of a more vital sense of origin than that which has been delivered to us through metaphysical and epistemological construction. The elucidation of this new sense of origin will require a broadened view of experience (thus a radicalization of empiricism) and an expanded concept of reason (thus a radicalization of rationalism). Our *epochē* of the conceptual schemes of metaphysical and epistemological construction will make possible an identification of the prejudice of epistemologically oriented thought itself as it moves out from a restricted perception of fact and a narrow conception of reason.

Our self-imposed requirement can be thusly summarized: a comprehension of the current crisis in man's understanding and interpretation of himself must take the route of a radical reflection that penetrates the presuppositions not only of scientific inquiry but also of philosophical analysis and construction, so that their origin can be disclosed. This requirement of radicality will install a posture of thought that is able to think to the "end" of philosophy itself. The "end of philosophy" is here to be understood not as the demise or elimination of philosophy, as it also in no way implies the demise or elimination of science. Nor is it to be understood in terms of the completion of philosophical thought along the lines of a fulfillment of the human potentialities of thought within a Hegelian scheme of absolute knowledge. Rather "end" designates the *limits* of a metaphysical and epistemological construction that has found its touchstone in categorial and methodological modes of thought. It is the awareness of these limits that most forcefully occasions the question of origin, requiring of reflection that it return to its primordial source. We could speak of this requirement for radical reflection as a species of "metaphilosophy" were it not for the conflicting significations that have become attached to this term. We propose therefore to speak of the *protophilosophical* and *protoscientific* character of radical reflection and hope that initially such a characterization will be a more appropriate index of the direction of our investigations and explorations.

Within the recent past a number of noteworthy studies on the origin and goal of the human sciences have been done, approaching the issue from a variety of philosophical perspectives. In *The Order of Things: An Archaeology of the Human Sciences,* Michel Foucault confronts the topic in a direct and straightforward manner from a neostructuralist position. In *The Crisis of European Sciences and Transcendental Phenomenology,* Edmund Husserl articulates the pertinent issues within the broader parameters of a search for the foundations of both the human and the natural sciences, making use of phenomenological procedures and insights. In *Knowledge and Human Interests,* Jürgen Habermas addresses similar concerns, admittedly in a somewhat more oblique manner, from the perspective of critical theory.

We will begin our investigation with a brief examination of the general design of these three approaches to the problem of the human sciences so as to place our own project within the wider context of current ruminations on the issue. This is not done simply to provide a species of "historical introduction" to our study. It comprises a more integral feature of our discussion insofar as our thesis to a great extent will be developed along the lines of a critical dialogue with the current representatives of structuralism, critical theory, and phenomenology.

Although disclaiming membership in any "Structuralist School," Michel Foucault employs an analytical framework which betrays a heavy structuralist influence. Within Foucault's scheme of things, the question of origin is posed as an issue of *archaeology.* He proposes an "archaeology of the human sciences." This archaeology is developed along the lines of an inquiry into the epistemic domains (*epistēmēs*) that provide the framework for an understanding of the different modes of discourse which at various times have been employed in the sciences of man. He attempts to identify four such epochal *epistēmēs* (late Middle Ages to late sixteenth century; seventeenth and eighteenth centuries; late eighteenth century to the early twentieth century; and the currently emerging one). These *epistēmēs* are neither to be understood as emanations of a cosmic scheme of things, nor as serial modifications of an enduring subject of history or substance of thought, nor as stages of a quiet unfolding of a unifying *telos* of history. They are characterized as ruptures, discontinuities, and disjunctions in the history of Western consciousness.[11] They simply appear, if you will, alongside one another. But an ordering is discernible in each of them, made possible by "discursive practice," so we can account for these ruptures amongst the *epistēmēs* by discerning the different manners in which language confers signification upon the world. The *epistēmēs* of the Middle Ages, the seventeenth and eighteenth centuries, and the nineteenth and twentieth centuries are distinguishable by the various uses of representational language; the decisiveness of the emerging *epistēmē* in the middle and late twentieth century consists in its emancipation from the representational model of language that provided the ordering principle in the preceding epochs.

At this time it is not our task to provide a detailed analysis of Foucault's comprehensive explanation of the emergence of the various *epistēmēs* in Western thought. We are interested more specifically in achieving some clarity in regard to his neostructuralist understanding and use of archaeology in raising the issue of the origin of the human sciences. Archaeology, for Foucault, replaces history. Hence, the question of the origin of the human sciences becomes for him a *nonhistorical* question. It is first of all a nonhistorical question in that it is not an interrogation of the diachronic development of the human sciences vis-à-vis the issues of historical causation, influence of traditions, and expressions of a *Zeitgeist*. Foucault's archaeology has nothing as such to do with a conventional history of ideas, which is intent upon laying out the continuities in the developing methodologies and achieved results of the various sciences of man. But his archaeology is nonhistorical in a more substantive sense, designed to displace the effort to historicize man himself, which received a dominant expression in the late nineteenth and early twentieth centuries. This later view of history, according to Foucault, "concerns man's very being, since he now realizes that he not only 'has history' all around him, but is himself, in his own historicity, that by means of which a history of human life, a history of economics, and a history of languages are given their form."[12] In short, Foucault rejects with one stroke the "historical consciousness" paradigm that was inaugurated by Hegel and proved to be so decisive in the development of modern Idealism.

The consequences of this rejection for Foucault are far-reaching. Not only does it result in a removal of the transcendental-empirical doublet, which is seen as but another expression of representational thought and language, but it also results in the dissolution of the historical subject himself. The new *epistémē* heralds the "death of man," displacing that philosophical anthropology of the nineteenth and early twentieth centuries which fashioned a philosophy of the *cogito* along the lines of an analytic of historicity. Thus Paul Ricoeur's general characterization of structuralism as "Kantianism without a transcendental subject"[13] takes on a peculiar aptness even in its application to Foucault. However, in the case of Foucault, it needs to be specified that what is dissolved is not only the transcendental subject but the historical subject as well. Indeed in the end, man himself is dissolved through a translation of the conditions for human subjectivity into the structure of language. Foucault concludes his *Order of Things* with a rhetorical question: "Since man was constituted at a time when language was doomed to dispersion, will he not be dispersed when language regains its unity? . . . Ought we not rather to give up thinking of man, or, to be more strict, to think of this disappearance of man—and the ground of possibility of all the sciences of man—as closely as possible in correlation with our concern with language?"[14]

Foucault's proposed archaeology of the human sciences shifts the focus of attention from the subject of consciousness and history (philosophical anthropology) to the "being of language." The origin of the human sciences is not to be found through ruminations on the nature of consciousness, historical existence, and the cultural life of man, but rather in the order of language. The sought-for *archē* is the passage of language through its various epistemic domains. And we must not forget that this is language without a speaker and without a socio-historical context. As Hayden White has suggestively formulated it, this is not the epiphany of the "Word made Flesh" but rather the epiphany, according to Saint Stephane Mallarmé, of the "Flesh made Word."[15] The history of man is transformed into a structure of language, and the *logos* of the *archē* of the human sciences is articulated through the deciphering of this structure without reference either to a universe of things or a community of subjects.

Thus we find in the neostructuralist thought of Foucault a bold and challenging doctrine of the origin of the human sciences. In our analysis and argumentation in the subsequent chapters, we will need to give some attention to his revolutionary proposal (found also in the literature of the mainstream structuralists) concerning the "death of man," which we will interpret to mean the dissolution of the historical subject of consciousness. In the course of our discussion, we will indicate some sympathies with Foucault's critical concerns and particularly as regards his dissatisfaction with the transcendental-empirical doublet; but we will also seize the opportunity to show that in the end Foucault's neostructuralist proposal (and that of structuralism more generally) provides the human sciences with a *misguided* archaeology.

The works of Edmund Husserl and particularly his last work, *The Crisis of European Sciences and Transcendental Phenomenology,* provide another noteworthy example of a contemporary exploration that probes the question of the origin and goal of the human sciences. In the thought of Husserl, the question of origin is posed within the context of historical reflections on the telos of Western philosophy. According to Husserl, Western philosophy as a teleology of reason has suffered a lapse into objectivism as a result of the pervasive influence of the Galilean ideal of mathematization. Galilean science (which Husserl is careful not to confuse with the procedures and results of Galileo's investigations) has produced a mathematized ontology of nature and a mathematized praxis. This *mathesis universalis* had profound consequences for the subsequent development of Western philosophy. It reached a decisive culmination in the rationalism of the Age of the Enlightenment and particularly in the philosophy of Leibniz. More recently it has made its presence felt in the various postures of contemporary positivism. The crisis of Western philosophy and Western science, according to Husserl, has its source in this recurring mathematization of nature and praxis, which occludes the origin of thought and action as it becomes manifest in a preobjective life-world. In succumbing to the ideal of an objective, mathematized, universal science of man and the world, philosophy and science alike have dissociated themselves from that praxis in the life-world in which practical interests, taken-for-granted knowledge, and ordinary language already register their significations. As a result Husserl's celebrated injunction for a *Rückgang auf die Lebenswelt* takes on not only a sense of importance but also a measure of radicality.

Thus, Husserl advises us to look to the life-world for the origin of the human sciences (as well as science more generally). It must be understood, however, that this project of returning to the life-world, involves neither an abandonment of philosophical reason nor a dissolution of objectivity in scientific inquiry. We must take Husserl seriously when he says, "I am certain that the European crisis has its roots in a misguided rationalism. But we must not take this to mean that rationality as such is evil or that it is of only subordinate significance for mankind's existence as a whole. Rationality, in that high and genuine sense of which alone we are speaking, in that primordial Greek sense which in the classical period of Greek philosophy had become an ideal, still requires, to be sure, much clarification through self-reflection; but it is called in its mature form to guide (our) development."[16]

What is at issue then is not rationality per se, but a rationality that has become "misguided" and has itself gravitated into a situation of crisis. Correspondingly, the indictment against science is not a condemnation of the ideals of objectivity and testability within the mathematical and physical sciences. What is at issue is the reductionism that follows in the wake of an attempted extension of positive science to a universal objective science that encompasses the domain of subjectivity. The ideal of positive science is itself a construct of subjectivity, never its foundation. This spirited attack on misguided rationalism and scientism does not, however, displace reason's obligation to penetrate and comprehend the structures of the life-world. The route of this reformed reason is the route of transcendental phenomenology. Admittedly, the transcendental phenomenology of the *Crisis* results in a modification of the "Cartesian way" to transcendental phenomenology as elaborated in Husserl's *Cartesian Meditations*. Yet, the general design of the earlier program of transcendental phenomenology remains intact, and Husserl never questioned its applicability in the formulation of an ontology of the life-world. Although an ontology of the order of a *mathesis universalis* is not possible, an ontology of the life-world, of the order of a transcendental-a priori science, is possible. "For the realm of souls there is in principle no such ontology, no science corresponding to the physicalistic-mathematical ideal, although psychic being is investigatable in transcendental universality, in a fully systematic way, and in principle in essential generality in the form of an a priori science."[17] Such an a priori science, proceeding via an *epochē* of the life-world, will exhibit an invariant structural framework of the life-world in which consciousness, temporality, spatiality, causality, and intersubjectivity can be understood in a preobjective manner.

The result of Husserl's investigation of the source of the crisis in Western philosophy and science and his analysis of the structures of the life-world is of inestimable value in helping us define our current project. We wish, however, to call attention to the fact that whereas the full title of Husserl's work which is devoted to an investigation of this issue is *The Crisis of European Sciences and Transcendental Phenomenology,* our investigation bears the title *Radical Reflection and the Origin of the Human Sciences.* The significance attaching to the different titles resides not merely with the scope of inquiry—our inquiry being more limited to the issue of origin as it pertains to the *human* sciences. The critical difference concerns the inquiry-standpoint of transcendental phenomenology, which remains the standpoint of Husserl even in this later work. Specifically, we are disposed to open up a friendly critique of Husserl's inquiry-standpoint on two points: (1) the continued employment of the metaphor of foundations and (2) the transcendental-phenomenological positioning of consciousness. These two issues are of particular relevance for our investigation of the origin of the sciences of man, as our subsequent explorations will show.

The use of the metaphor of foundations invites a disturbing self-arrogation on the part of philosophy. It prompts the presumption that philosophical reason is able to establish in a definitive way the epistemic and ontologic basis or ground for the "truth" of the special sciences of man. In Husserl's transcendental phenomenology, the foundation metaphor is a modified continuation of the Cartesian metaphor in which metaphysics functions as the roots, which nourish the trunk (physics as a study of nature), from which in turn the special sciences branch off. Admittedly, in Husserl's inquiry-standpoint transcendental phenomenology replaces Cartesian metaphysics as the genuine goal of philosophy, and the study of nature is pruned of the Galilean ideal of mathematization which continued to inform the reflections of Descartes. Yet, philosophical reflection is still defined as a search for the foundations, and on this point a thread of continuity throughout Husserl's intellectual development is discernible.

In his earlier writings, Husserl is principally interested in establishing the foundations of mathematics, logic, and theory of knowledge. In his later writings, he moves to an interrogation of the foundations of culture and history via his explorations of a transcendental-phenomenological "ontology of the life-world." We are critically concerned about the foundation-claim within such a program and the effect of such a claim on the communicative performance between philosophy and the special sciences of man. Is it possible to redefine the problem of origin in such a way that it becomes an issue for philosophy and the human sciences within a communicative reciprocity of common reflection and investigation? Or must philosophy perennially reaffirm its squatter's rights and demand of the special sciences that any fundamental thinking be left to it? Is philosophy destined to reflect on the foundations, and are the special human sciences destined to observe the facts? Or may there be a possibility of reasking the question of origin in such a manner that the commonly accepted bifurcation of reflection on meaning and observation of fact is reexamined and undercut? These, and similar interrogations, will direct our inquiry in the following chapters.

The second critical question that we wish to place before Husserl concerns the continuing epistemic and ontologic weight that is distributed to consciousness. His phenomenology, up to the very end, remains a philosophy of consciousness, and in this we can detect the permanent deposit that classical German idealism left in his thinking. Consciousness is redefined as intentional from bottom up; yet, the idealistic requirement for grounding evidence in a self-reflexive consciousness remains intact, and its conditions can only be met through the use of a sharp distinction between the transcendental and the empirical. No foundations can be found in the domain of empirical consciousness. A transcendental-phenomenological reduction of the merely empirical is required, thus bringing into view the domain of transcendental consciousness and its interstices of intentionality. This transcendental consciousness in its privileged moment of self-reflexivity affords the sought after origin and foundation of the natural and the human sciences. Again, we submit to critical inquiry the alleged requirement for a self-reflexivity that is modeled after an idealistically oriented search for the transcendental conditions of knowledge. Might not the question of the origin of the human sciences be more productively pursued within the framework of a radical reflection on *prescientific* and *prephilosophical* thought and praxis? Such a reflection would demand an eventual dismantling of the idealistic opposition of the transcendental and the empirical.

Now it would appear that Jürgen Habermas and the proponents of the school of critical theory have incisively addressed some of the problem areas that we have found in Husserl's attempt to diagnose and resolve the current crisis in the Western sciences, both of man and nature. Is not the thrust of the critique of critical theory projected in the direction of a much more radical interrogation of the resources of philosophical reason than Husserl himself ever entertained, thus confirming our suspicion that the metaphor of philosophical foundations needs to be re-thought? Is not the emphasis by the critical theorists on the in-sinuation of interest and praxis-oriented reflection into the designs of theory construction a timely and cogent counterplay? Does not the accentuated appeal by Habermas and his interpret-ers to the importance of sociological, anthropological, psychoanalytical, and political analysis open the path to a fresh approach to the question of the origin and possible unification of the sciences of man? We are disposed to answer these questions in the affirmative and thus recognize that in inducing us to ask these questions the proponents of critical theory have provided us with a legacy that is of considerable value. Yet, the specific analyses and formulations with respect to the issues of cognition and interest and the role of the human and the natural sciences in the cultural life of man that are set forth in the corpus of critical theory them-selves require the test of critical judgment.

Assuredly, Habermas's critique of science is more radical than that of Husserl, leading Habermas to a radicalization of Husserl's phenomenological inquiry-standpoint. Habermas finds all science, both that of nature and of man, subject to the illusion of pure theory, cut off from its roots in the domain of human interest, and thus placed in a position of being unable to understand itself. A grievous and unhappy consequence of this, according to Habermas, is that the designs and achievements of science become aligned with the productive forces and bureaucratic powers at work in society at large, carrying with them a considerable amount of ideological residue, culminating in a state of affairs in which the claims for a pure science become infected with a species of false consciousness. What is required to counteract this crisis of misunderstanding on the part of science, according to Habermas, is a critical theory of knowledge, proceeding from Hegel's radicalization of Kant, wherewith the meaning of science itself can first be placed into question.

Concerning the matter of Habermas's specific criticism of Husserl's attempt to provide a foundation for the sciences, it can be said that Habermas finds Husserl guilty of a misconception of the crisis in human science and human knowledge more gener-ally. This misconception, according to Habermas, follows from Husserl's acceptance of a traditional concept of knowledge, of a purely contemplative sort, which still conceals the proper link be-tween theory and human interests. Although sympathetic with Husserl's attack on positivism, Habermas argues that Husserl fails to see the sub rosa connection between the positivism that he re-jects and the ontology of knowledge that he accepts.

> His mistake is due to his failure to see through the connection
> between positivism, which he rightly criticizes, and the kind of
> ontology which he unwittingly derives from the traditional concept
> of theory. . . . The mistake is obvious: theory in the traditional sense
> was related to life because of its claim to having discovered the
> paradigm of order in Nature and man. It was only in this, its
> cosmological role, that Theoria had the power at the same time to
> orient action. But just for this reason Husserl ought not to expect
> educational processes to emerge from a phenomenology which has
> transcendentally purged the old theory of its cosmological content,
> and which consequently merely sticks to something like a theoretical
> attitude in an abstract kind of way.[18]

We have cited Habermas's criticism of Husserl at some length
not only because it brings to light a conceptual issue which requires some attention, but also because it provides an interesting
example of a misreading of Husserl. Clearly the former is of more
consequence than the latter. When Habermas criticizes Husserl
for finding the crisis of the European sciences in their detachment
from the classical concept of theory rather than in their inability
to finally become liberated from the classical theory itself, an important insight is generated at the expense of Husserl becoming
the proverbial straw man. It is surely, in this day, untenable to
saddle Husserl with that classical concept of theory that became
normative for the Greek philosophical mind. To speak, as does
Habermas, of a concept of theory and ontology of knowledge
"which underlies philosophy from Plato up to Husserl"[19] is to mix
much that should remain separate. Although there have been
some intermittent attempts to uncover the "Platonism" of Husserl,
these attempts are all aborted in the recognition that Husserl's
transcendentally determined knowledge is not the divinely inspired *epistēmē* of Plato, and that the essences of which Husserl
speaks have nothing to do with the eternal, cosmological ar-
chetypes of Plato's theory of ideas. As we have seen, Husserl in
the *Crisis* does speak of the primordial Greek sense of rationality,
particularly as it is expressed in the Greek's sense of wonder
($\Theta\alpha\upsilon\mu\alpha\zeta\epsilon\iota\nu$), but this is to be confused neither with the theory
construction at work in Plato's celebrated doctrine of ideas nor
with Aristotle's philosophy of substance. Hence, Habermas's ascription of an underlying Platonist theory of knowledge and
metaphysics to Husserl's transcendental phenomenology cannot
stand the test of careful scrutiny.

Yet, the conceptual issues which Habermas raises in his critique
of Husserl are of considerable import. Although we would want to
exonerate Husserl from the charge of Platonism, we agree that

Habermas's demand for a radicalization of the Kantian perspective of a transcendental grounding of scientific knowledge—which continued to inform Husserl's search for the foundations—is well placed. It is a curious consequence of Kant's critical philosophy that it should remain so uncritical with respect to basic points of presupposition. Kant simply assumes that mathematics and physics (and more specifically of a Newtonian stripe) provide paradigms of scientific knowledge, thus defining the transcendental question as one which interrogates the conditions of their possibility. The status of mathematics and physics as paradigmatic instances of veridical knowledge is never called into question, and hence the issue of what it is that counts as science is never critically formulated. This is the issue, among others, that Habermas forcefully calls to our attention, and it is an issue which would seem to require the services of some form of a critical theory of knowledge.

At the very point, however, at which Habermas raises our hopes for a fresh approach to knowledge and social reality, we are disappointed to find that he himself remains very "traditionalist," particularly vis-à-vis his appeal to a transcendental framework of inquiry as the philosophical foundation for the unification of cognition and interests. In *Knowledge and Human Interests,* Habermas himself proceeds from a variation of that transcendental self-reflection which he finds so baneful in the philosophy of Husserl. Admittedly, transcendental reflection undergoes a conceptual sea-change when it becomes a servant to critical theory of knowledge. Habermas is intent on uniting cognition and interest at the very base of transcendental self-reflection, and thus purports to avoid that purely contemplative attitude that he still ascribes to Husserl. Interests guide cognition—in the domain of empirical natural science, in the domain of the historical human sciences, and most decisively in the domain of the psychoanalytic critique of knowledge. It is specifically in the latter domain that the interlacing of cognition and interest (in the guise of emancipatory interest) becomes explicit.

In the end this all yields a transcendental philosophical anthropology which purports to give an account of man's socio-historical self-formative process within a transcendental framework of cognitive interests. This transcendental philosophical anthropology has occasioned vigorous counterattacks, interestingly enough, by empiricists and idealists alike. Empiricists, particularly of the positivist camp, indict Habermas for transgressing the limits of empirical knowledge in an appeal to nonverifiable transcendental conditions. Idealists, particularly of the

Kantian persuasion, attack Habermas for corroding the purity of transcendental knowledge by blending it with the natural genesis of human needs, interests, and activities.[20] These counterattacks hardly come as a total surprise. So long as the traditional dichotomies of empirical vs. transcendental, a posteriori vs. a priori, and contingent vs. necessary inform one's inquiry-standpoint in addressing the interplay of knowledge and interest, one remains open to the charge of doing a disservice to the sedimented and accepted significations of the polarized concepts within the inquiry-standpoint and inviting an eel-like eclecticism of quasi-transcendental and quasi-empirical knowledge determinants.

Thus, when all is said and done, it would seem that Habermas's own diagnosis and proposed cure for the existing crisis of misunderstanding that issues from an illusion of pure theory falls prey to a crisis of its own—a crisis of concepts within an inquiry-standpoint that uncritically legitimates the transcendental-empirical framework of question posing. Habermas has incisively pinpointed the illusion of objectivity that attaches to the alleged pure theory of classical, cosmologically oriented reflection; however, he has not been able to resist, at least in his earlier writings, the lure of the sirens of the modern Charybdis of transcendental reflection on the one hand and the Scylla of empirical fact on the other. Indeed, the framework of his transcendental philosophical anthropology continues to be nurtured by this opposition.

It should be noted, however, that Habermas himself has become increasingly dissatisfied with some of his earlier attempts to formulate a transcendental philosophical anthropology and has turned his attention to a more linguistic and rhetoric oriented approach to a critical theory of knowledge. It were as though he became more and more cognizant of the uncritical features of the conceptual framework which he designed in *Knowledge and Human Interests*. C. K. Lenhardt, for example, speaks of a "veritable *coupure épistémolgique*" that is discernible in Habermas's later shift from transcendental anthropology to a theory of communicative competence.[21]

Along the lines of the later reflections of Habermas on matters of language and communication, the very important work of Karl-Otto Apel should be mentioned. More incisively than any other representative of the critical theory school, Apel has grasped the complexity and import of the problematic at issue. Highly sensitive to the need to rethink the meaning and use of the transcendental posture, he has developed a *transcendental pragmatic of language* in which the traditional Kantian as well as Husserlian understanding of transcendental is refashioned in the guise of a grounding of discourse within the pragmatic dimension of argumentative language use. This refashioning of transcendental reflection is designed to yield the pragmatic conditions for the possibility of intersubjectively valid knowledge and a consensus theory of truth.[22] In Apel's modified reappropriation of the meaning of transcendental, the troublesome (for both Kant and Husserl) regression to a transcendental ego is displaced; and the limitations of Husserl's theory of evidence as evidence for an intending consciousness are brought to light. The question of validity is reformulated in terms of an intersubjective validation of arguments within a Peircian-type community of investigators and interpreters.

The achievements of Apel's projected reform of the transcendental, and we might say the reform of modern theory of knowledge from Descartes to Husserl, are seminal and noteworthy. Apel has made a possible case for the transcendental within the ruminations of a reconstructed critical theory of knowledge. Unfortunately, however, the problem is circumscribed within the framework of a theory of knowledge and a theory of discourse which finds its paradigm in the language and procedures of argumentation. Although this framework may be adequate for the fulfillment of Apel's legitimate requirement for a "serious metascientific analysis of the relations between science and the humanities,"[23] it stops short of the equally important mandate for a disciplined *protophilosophical* exploration of the origin of the human sciences. This mandate takes on a measure of urgency in the moment that one recognizes that not all language takes the form of argumentative competence, used in the service of securing the foundations for a theory of knowledge. The nonargumentative uses of language in gestural signification, performative utterances, and mytho-poetic disclosure also play a role in what we shall explicate as the origin of the sciences of man, which will then first provide the vantage point from which to address the question of the relation of the sciences and the humanities. To come to grips with the issue of origin, a broader notion of the logos of language than that supplied by critical theory is required.

We have looked briefly at three current explanations of the crisis in the human sciences (the neostructuralism of Foucault, the transcendental phenomenology of Husserl, and the critical theory of Habermas and Apel), each in its own way raising the question of origin. We have registered their positive contributions toward a definition of the issue at hand, and we have suggested some preliminary criticisms of their proposed solutions. In the subsequent

chapters, much of what we will have to say will take the form of a
critical dialogue with some of the representatives of structuralism,
phenomenology, and critical theory. But also we will make an effort to work out the motivations and limitations of a scientific and
philosophical study of man afresh, hopefully in such a manner
that the shortcomings of the common current approaches are
rectified. In our effort to engender a grasp of the origin of the
sciences of man, wherewith the current crisis can at once be understood and overcome, we will begin with an analysis of the project of philosophical anthropology and through the use of the
resources of radical reflection lay out the necessity for a radicalization of reflection on the being and behavior of man. Structuralism, phenomenology, and critical theory as they address the
topic of the sciences of man have not yet fully succeeded in free-
ing their framework of inquiry from the presuppositions of classical, idealistically oriented philosophical anthropology. Even the
structuralists pronouncement of the "death of man" is shaped by
the inquiry-standpoint of philosophical anthropology, of which it
is an alleged antagonist. Therefore, we must begin anew, locate
where the issue has been placed by philosophical anthropology,
and through radical critique work our way back to the origin of
scientific and philosophical investigations of the behavior and
being of man.

NOTES

1. Although there are certain areas in the biological sciences which relate
quite specifically to issues in the human sciences, the present study is
more directly concerned with the idea of the science of man as it surfaces
in the investigations of the psychological, social, and historical sciences.
We will consider some of the contributions of the biological sciences via
the impact that they have had in the development of what is commonly
referred to as "biological philosophical anthropology." This development
includes the contributions of A. Gehlen, A. Portmann, Jakob von
Uexküll, F. J. J. Buytendijk, Helmut Plessner, and others. For a general
discussion of the designs of biological philosophical anthropology the
reader is referred to H. O. Pappé's entry, "Philosophical Anthropology"
in *Encyclopedia of Philosophy,* ed. Paul Edwards (New York: Macmillan Co.,
1967), Vol. 6, pp. 162–63.

2. Harold D. Lasswell, *Power and Personality* (New York: W. W. Norton &
Co., 1948); Ralf Dahrendorf, *Homo Sociologicus* (Opladen: Westdeutscher
Verlag, 1972); Ernst Cassirer, *An Essay on Man* (New Haven: Yale
University Press, 1944); Johan Huizinga, *Homo Ludens* (Boston: Beacon

Press, 1962); Gabriel Marcel, *Homo Viator* (Aubier: Editions Montaigne, 1944); Roland Barthes, *Critical Essays*, trans. R. Howard (Evanston: Northwestern University Press, 1972); Philip Rieff, *Freud: The Mind of the Moralist* (New York: Doubleday, 1959); and Edward Farley, *Ecclesial Man* (Philadelphia: Fortress Press, 1975).

3. Ralf Dahrendorf, *Essays in the Theory of Society* (Stanford: University Press, 1968). In this work in particular Dahrendorf takes pains to distinguish *homo sociologicus* as "scientific man" from concretely existing man: "Man as the bearer of social roles is not primarily a description of reality, but a scientific construct," p. 25.

4. *Man's Place in Nature*, trans. Hans Meyerhoff (New York: The Noonday Press, 1961), pp. 4, 5–6.

5. *An Essay on Man* (New Haven: Yale University Press, 1944), p. 22.

6. "The Ambiguity of the Sciences of Man," *Diogenes*, No. 26, 1959, p. 52.

7. "The Antinomy of Human Reality and the Problem of Philosophical Anthropology," *Readings in Existential Phenomenology*, eds. N. Lawrence and D. O'Connor (Englewood Cliffs: Prentice-Hall, Inc., 1967), p. 390.

8. *Studies in Ethnomethodology* (Englewood Cliffs: Prentice-Hall, Inc., 1967). Norman Birnbaum has addressed the issue of a naive over-extension of techniques of quantification in the name of empiricism, and has correctly concluded that: "There is no epistemological or practical warrant for assigning a privileged place to inquiries entailing interviews or direct observations rather than the utilization of other types of data. In particular, historical inquiries are neither less nor more 'empirical' than other kinds. The insistence of some that the term 'empirical' be restricted to quantitative work on contemporary population is easy enough to explain, but difficult to excuse." *Toward a Critical Sociology* (Oxford University Press, 1971), p. 123. The reader is also referred to A. V. Cicourel's discussion of the problems of measurement which result from a naïve restriction of measurement to mathematical models in his book, *Method and Measurement in Sociology* (Glencoe: The Free Press, 1964).

9. See particularly his book, *Beyond Freedom and Dignity* (New York: Alfred A. Knopf, 1971).

10. Martin Heidegger, more than any other contemporary thinker, has been concerned to elucidate and put into perspective the history of metaphysics as a history of the application of a categorial scheme (in which substance and causality play a privileged role), in which an explicit metaphysical view of origin is utilized. In the end, according to Heidegger, such a project is destined to conceal the primordial source of questioning and thinking because it follows the path of an investigation of

beings (entities) and their varied relations, objectifying both within a
categorial scheme, and thus occluding the originative presence of Being.
(See particularly his essay, "The Way Back into the Ground of
Metaphysics," trans. W. Kaufman, *Existentialism from Dostoevsky to Sartre*
(New York: Meridian Books, 1956); and his work, *Identity and Difference,*
trans. J. Stambaugh (New York: Harper and Row, 1969). Heidegger's
reflections, particularly in his later period, are geared to a reminiscence
of Being that provides a disclosure of and return to the beginnings. This
reminiscence follows the path of explorations of originative thinking at
work in art, poetry, and language itself. (See particularly his essay, "The
Origin of the Work of Art," trans. A. Hofstadter in *Poetry, Language,
Thought* (New York: Harper and Row, 1971); and his work, *Unterwegs Zur
Sprache,* (Tübingen: Günther Neske Pfullingen, 1959).

11. Hayden V. White, in his illuminating discussion of Foucault in his
article, "Foucault Decoded: Notes from Underground" in *History and
Thought,* XII, 1973, appopriately remarks that "The imagery used to
characterize the epochs is not that of a 'river of time' or 'flow of
consciousness,' but that of an 'archipelago,' a chain of epistemic islands,
the deepest connections among which are unknown—and unknowable,"
p. 28.

12. *The Order of Things: An Archaeology of the Human Sciences* (New York:
Vintage Books, 1973), p. 370.

13. *The Conflict of Interpretations: Essays in Hermeneutics,* ed. Don Ihde
(Evanston: Northwestern University Press, 1974), p. 52.

14. *The Order of Things,* p. 386.

15. "Foucault Decoded: Notes from Underground," p. 53.

16. *The Crisis of European Sciences and Transcendental Phenomenology,* trans.
David Carr (Evanston: Northwestern University Press, 1970), p. 290.

17. *The Crisis,* p. 265.

18. "Knowledge and Interest," *Sociological Theory and Philosophical
Analysis,* eds. Dorothy Emmet and Alasdair MacIntyre (New York:
Macmillan, 1970), pp. 41–42.

19. "Knowledge and Interest," p. 39.

20. Fred R. Dallmayr provides us with a perceptive analysis of these and
other criticisms of Habermas's transcendental philosophical anthropology
in his article, "Critical Theory Criticized: Habermas's *Knowledge and
Human Interests* and its Aftermath" in *Philosophy of the Social Sciences,* Vol.
2, No. 3, 1972.

21. "The Rise and Fall of Transcendental Anthropology" in *Philosophy of the Social Sciences,* Vol. 2, No. 3, 1972.

22. See particularly his article, "The Problem of Philosophical Fundamental-Grounding in Light of a Transcendental Pragmatic of Language," *Man and World,* Vol. 8, No. 3, 1975. Also see his article, *"Zur Idee einer transzendentalen Sprachpragmatik"* in *Aspekte und Probleme der Sprachphilosophie,* ed. J. Simon (Freiburg: Verlag Alber, 1974).

23. "The A Priori of Communication and the Foundation of the Humanities," *Man and World,* Vol. 5, No. 1, 1972, p. 3.

CHAPTER 2

From Philosophical Anthropology to Radical Anthropological Reflection

Philosophical anthropology, in its most inclusive sense, is the philosophical study of man. Such a very general characterization, however, packs into the project of philosophical thropology a rather enormous and encompassing scope of inquiry. It includes everything that every philosopher has said about the being and behavior of man. It encompasses, for example, Plato's theory of the tripartite psyche, Aquinas's doctrine of the soul as the spiritual form of the human body, Descartes's argument for a dualism of material and mental substance, Fichte's view of the ego as pure act, Hume's proposal that the self is a bundle of perceptions, Sartre's notion of man as a useless passion—and a great deal more. Such a very general and all-inclusive characterization of philosophical anthropology as the philosophical study of man may, of course, possess its intrinsic merit. Our interests, however, move in the direction of a more specific delineation of the design and concerns of philosophical anthropology. This specific delineation will make it possible, first of all, to distinguish philosophical anthropology from pre-Kantian "speculative psychology," in which there was a rather bold and uncritical application of the traditional metaphysical schemata of substance and attributes, form and matter, essence and existence, in an effort to designate an invariant nature of man. Further, it will hopefully provide a clarification of the parameters of philosophical anthropology as a special discipline shaped by specific developments in modern philosophy and the more recent emergence of the human sciences. We will then be in position to discern the peculiar problematic that has been posed by the confrontation of a modern philosophical anthropology of knowledge with the developing special sciences of man and, in response to this problematic, suggest a radicalization of the project of philosophical anthropology itself. This will mark our move from philosophical anthropology as a special discipline to a radical anthropological reflection.

29

Our delineation of the idea and scope of philosophical anthropology as a specialized discipline within modern philosophical thought must begin with Kant. Not only did he author a book bearing the specific title *Anthropology from a Pragmatic Point of View*,[1] but he also dealt with various topics of philosophical anthropology throughout the rest of his works, and particularly in his *Introduction to Logic*. Pragmatic anthropology, as Kant defines it in his *Anthropology*, comprises an empirical body of knowledge. In no sense, however, is this to be understood as a simple serialization of empirical observations about human behavior. The framework of inquiry in which the empirics of human thought and action are addressed is precisely that of the apriori and transcendental principles of his critical philosophy. Already here the lines of demarcation between pure and empirical knowledge are drawn, and in the end it is the principles of pure philosophy that provide the framework for the unification and integration of anthropological observations and insights relating to feeling, volition, cognition, wit, genius, freedom, personality, temperment, race, sex, and cultural achievement.

This framework of inquiry is continued in Kant's later reflections on anthropology in his *Introduction to Logic*, which appeared in 1800. However, in this later work a privilege is conferred upon the anthropological question "What is man?" that is not made explicit in his earlier work. After defining philosophy as "the science of the relation of all knowledge and every use of reason to the ultimate end of human reason, to which, as supreme, all other ends are subordinated, and must be combined into unity in it,"[2] Kant summarizes the basic questions cutting across the field of philosophy with four interrelated interrogations: What can I know? What ought I to do? What may I hope? What is man? Commenting on these questions Kant informs us: "The first question is answered by *Metaphysics*, the second by *Morals*, the third by *Religion*, and the fourth by *Anthropology*. In reality, however, all these might be reckoned under anthropology, since the first three questions refer to the last."[3] An effort must be made to discern the relevance of Kant's inquiries in his three *Critiques* and his book on religion to a philosophical anthropology which first provides the thematic matrix in which the a priori principles of knowledge and moral action, the role of the aesthetic imagination, and the significations of religious experience find their foundation.[4]

Although it may well be the case, as Heidegger has argued in his book *Kant and the Problem of Metaphysics*, that Kant never fully succeeded in carrying out his proposed project of laying the foundations for metaphysics and a theory of morals through the services of a critical philosophical anthropology; yet, the fact remains that the destiny of any future philosophical anthropology was shaped by Kant's reflections. Henceforth it was to take on the determination of *critical* philosophical anthropology. Kant's demonstration of the ineradicable limits of human reason, which issue from the finitude of human existence, has effectively precluded any future, dogmatic, precritical metaphysics of man. Not only the limitation of theoretical reason in its drive toward the unification of the objective and subjective conditions of experience, but also the limitation of pure practical reason as it confronts the resilient, wayward inclinations and passions in the life of the moral self find their source in the finitude of man. The emerging philosophical anthropology thus proceeded along the lines of a philosophy of human finitude.

In the course of its development this new discipline became heir to other philosophically formative influences of considerable importance, and particularly the influence stemming from the philosophy of Hegel. Hegel accepted Kant's standpoint of critical inquiry and then proceeded to radicalize it. The determining conditions for the possibility of knowledge for Hegel are no longer set by the grammar and the apperceptive synthesis operative in the judgments of the mathematical and the physical sciences, but now find their genealogy in a historical consciousness striving for self-comprehension. For Hegel the mathematical and physical sciences do not, as they did for Kant, provide the paradigmatic instances of knowledge; they are themselves derivative from a more foundational historical science. The effect of this explicit historization of knowledge on the subsequent designs of philosophical anthropology was far-reaching. It finally resulted in the shifting of the focus from the transcendental subject to the historical subject and in the redefining of the anthropology of knowledge as an articulation of the structures of historical self-understanding. Hegelian philosophical anthropology thus defines the central project as one of critical reflection on the formative factors in man's process of historical self-development, a process which takes the path of the actualization of freedom. It was this account of the historicity of consciousness and the accompanying drive toward freedom that occasioned, both by positive and negative response, the development of post-Hegelian *concrete* anthropology—in Feuerbach, Marx, existentialism, and French humanism.

The development of the discipline of philosophical anthropology was shaped not only by the Kantian, Hegelian, and post-Hegelian developments in modern and nineteenth-century philosophical thought; it was also shaped by the development and proliferation of the various human sciences—psychology, sociology, cultural anthropology, political economy, and international law. Whereas the speculative psychology of traditional metaphysics could enjoy a conceptual insularity insofar as it antedated the emergence of the special sciences of man, philosophical anthropology was destined to develop *with* the newly founded sciences and could not avoid the challenges that they presented. Indeed, these developing special sciences, with their accelerated accumulation of information, began to play a role in the very definition of the task and scope of philosophical anthropology. It is not surprising, therefore, to find the following definition of philosophical anthropology, formulated by H. O. Pappé, in the current edition of the *Encyclopedia of Philosophy:*

> Philosophical anthropology seeks to interpret philosophically the facts that the sciences have discovered concerning the nature of man and of the human condition. . . . [It] seeks to correlate the various anthropologies that have developed with the specialization of the sciences. . . . In order to stem what its followers describe as anarchy of thought and the 'loss of the center', *philosophical anthropology offers itself as a coordinating discipline.*[5] (Italics mine).

A remarkably similar definition is supplied by Jürgen Habermas in his entry in the *Fisher-Lexicon: Philosophie,* the German counterpart to the Anglo-American *Encyclopedia of Philosophy.* In his characterization of the discipline, Habermas writes: "Philosophical anthropology assimilates and integrates the findings of those sciences—like psychology, sociology, archaeology, and linguistics—that deal with man and his achievements . . . from which a philosophical interpretation of the results of the special sciences is to proceed."[6]

Both Pappé and Habermas in their lexical definitions succeed in articulating the notable impact of the special human sciences on philosophical anthropology in the developing self-understanding of its task. The proliferation and advance of knowledge in the special human sciences installed a new requirement for philosophical anthropology, namely, that of coordinating the facts and findings of these special sciences and interpreting the results in a philosophical manner. Clearly the demands for the fulfillment of this requirement soon became staggering, given the exponential growth of information in the special sciences and the concomitant broadening of the scope of philosophical anthropology. Given this state of affairs, it is quite natural that a division of conceptual labor would take place, sectioning philosophical anthropology off into the complementing subdisciplines of biological philosophical anthropology, psychological philosophical anthropology, cultural philosophical anthropology, and theological philosophical anthropology. The representatives of each of these subdisciplines addressed themselves to the peculiar problems posed for philosophical analysis and interpretation by the developing knowledge in the disciplines of biology, psychology, sociology, and theology.[7]

Philosophical anthropology as a branch of philosophical study has been defined principally through the convergence of the formative philosophical influences stemming from Kant and Hegel, on the one hand, and the scientific advances in the special sciences on the other. Admittedly the formative philosophical influences have not exemplified a uniform and continuous ideational fabric—particularly in the development of post-Hegelian thought—nor have the emerging human sciences registered an identical challenge to every participating philosophical anthropologist. However, in spite of the variegated postures assumed by this relatively new branch of philosophical study, the Kantian and Hegelian frameworks of inquiry continued to inform the course of its development throughout. Kantian and Hegelian modes of thought left such an impress on all subsequent anthropological reflection that they were discernible even in the thought of the philosophers who were inclined to attack these modes of thought. Subsequent philosophical anthropologists were destined to use Kant's and Hegel's concepts even when they attacked their philosophical doctrines, as is particularly evident in the case of Marx and the existentialists.

We will now make an effort to isolate some of the pivotal motifs in the tradition of philosophical anthropology as they pertain particularly to the issue of crisis in the current sciences of man, and in doing so we hope to make visible the requirement for a radicalization of this tradition so as to forge an access to the origin of both philosophical reflection and scientific investigation pertinent to the being and behavior of man. This effort at radicalization will take as its point of departure a critical analysis of the contributions of Feuerbach and Marx and the contemporary structuralist response to these contributions.

We could well speak of the legacy of Kantian and Hegelian philosophical anthropology as the debut of the centrality of the subject. In both Kant and Hegel, we observe the shift from substance to subject. The principal epochal feature of their combined thought marks the coming to age of the subject. In Kant's critical philosophy, this subject appears first in the guise of the transcendental ego, in which the synthesis of sensibility and understanding is accomplished. The consciousness of this transcendental ego is still projected toward the object, the common charges of subjectivism in Kant's theory of knowledge notwithstanding. Admittedly, the synthesis of sensibility and understanding is accomplished by the subject, but only insofar as consciousness works with the given object. The achievement of synthesis requires the external mediation of the "thing-in-itself" as given object for consciousness, an achievement which finds its pivot in the operation of the transcendental imagination, which Kant repeatedly characterizes as a "blind but indispensable" function of the soul. Within this transcendental perspective, then, the subject as consciousness is principally "outer-directed." It does not follow the path of a reflexive return upon itself. It takes on a referential rather than a self-reflexive determination.

However, in this synthesis accomplished through a reference to the object, an implicit self-reflexivity of consciousness is already prefigured by the requirement for an explanation of the objectivity of the object rendered possible by the projective thrust of consciousness. Reference to objects requires a power within consciousness whereby it is able to open itself to the appearances and receive them as objects. Although Kant does not render explicit the self-reflexivity of consciousness in his doctrine of the transcendental ego in the first *Critique,* he approaches it much more closely with his doctrine of the moral self in the second *Critique,* where the project inevitably takes us to "persons" rather than "things." Whereas the synthesis of theoretical reason requires only an oblique adumbration of the self-reflexive structure of consciousness, the synthesis of practical reason requires the projection of a task in which the achievement of the moral posture demands self-knowledge, self-control, and self-realization.[8]

It was in the philosophical systems of Fichte and Hegel, however, that the subject as self-reflexive consciousness received a more decisive expression and became enshrined as an essential feature of classical German Idealism. Self-reflexivity is viewed by Fichte principally as a voluntaristic event, operative within the interiority of the pure *act,* which for Fichte always precedes the *word.* Hegel confers on self-reflexivity a more intellectualistic comportment, linking it more directly with self-consciousness and the achievement of self-knowledge by Spirit. "The self-contained existence of Spirit," says Hegel, "is none other than self-consciousness—consciousness of one's own being. Two things must be distinguished in consciousness; first, the fact *that I know;* secondly, *what I know.* In *self* consciousness they are merged in

one: for Spirit *knows itself*."⁹ This rather bold application of the
principle of self-reflexive consciousness not only provided the central motif for Hegel's dialectical idealism but it also helped
prepare the stage for the development of a philosophical anthropology of knowledge in which the theoretical act of self-
reflexive consciousness was granted a peculiar privilege.

The paramount importance of this theoretical self-reflexivity of
consciousness for the history of philosophical anthropology is
readily discernible in the thought of Ludwig Feuerbach, who has
been named by one of his translators and interpreters as "the
philosophical anthropologist *par excellence*."¹⁰ Feuerbach's analysis
of the essence of man proceeds from the principle of an abstract
self-reflexivity of consciousness in which consciousness is directed
to itself as an object of thought. This object of thought, understood as infinite and unlimited, is for Feuerbach the mark of
man's essential nature. "Consciousness in the strictest sense is present only in a being to whom his species, his essential nature, is an
object of thought. . . . Consciousness, in the strict or proper sense,
is identical with consciousness of the infinite; a limited consciousness is no consciousness; consciousness is essentially infinite in nature."¹¹ The idealist heritage of Hegel clearly remains intact in
Feuerbach's philosophy of man. Indeed, it is carried to a somewhat surprising and unexpected fulfillment. The final stage of
Absolute Spirit, memorialized in Hegel's system, achieves incar-
nation in the essence of man. The power of thought in its self-
reflexive operation overcomes its finitude and posits itself as the
true Absolute. Self-reflexive consciousness is the vehicle by which
thought is able to reflect on itself as the presence of the Divine in
the human.

What interests us at this juncture is the manifold exemplifications and uses of the idealist model of self-reflexive consciousness
in the Hegelian and post-Hegelian tradition of philosophical anthropology. Philosophical anthropology in the guise of a
"philosophy of consciousness" conferred upon this model the
privilege of an absolute presupposition. Consciousness, we
learned from Hegel, is imbued with the power of grasping itself as
its own object. Thus the self-reflexivity operative in such
phenomena as self-knowledge, self-affirmation, self-love, self-
hate, and self-pity is a reflexivity wherewith consciousness in its
theoretical mode can establish the unimpeachable ground or
foundation of all thought and action. Feuerbach, as we have seen,
appropriates this insight of Hegel and puts it to use in his designs
of an atheistic theology. Marx, the professed and resolute anti-
Hegelian, was also unable to free himself in his early writings

from this model of reflexive self-consciousness in his effort to lay the foundations for a concrete philosophy of man. His notion of "species-being," which plays such a dominant role in his early theory of alienated labor, carried the imprint of both Hegel and Feuerbach. Indeed, Marx simply borrowed the term, "species-being," from Feuerbach's *The Essence of Christianity* and retrenched it so as to fit his description of the self-alienation at work in capitalistic society. But the model of self-reflexive consciousness remains intact, clearly evidenced when Marx writes: "Conscious life activity distinguishes man from the life activity of animals. Only for this reason is he a species-being. Or rather, he is only a self-conscious being, i.e., his own life is an object for him, because he is a species-being."[12]

In this way Marx's philosophical anthropology, like that of his predecessors, moves out from the primacy of consciousness in its mode of self-reflexivity. Herein resides the Hegelian and Feuerbachian legacy within Marx's own thought, and his early reflections on alienated labor and the nature of man as species-being are intelligible only when seen against the background of this legacy. Yet a decisive moment in Marx's internal critique of this idealist legacy concerns his effort to move beyond the theoretical and abstract self-reflexivity of consciousness so as to reinsert consciousness into the density of concrete relationships of life, labor, and history. This suggested reorientation of the classical model of theoretical, self-reflexive consciousness is articulated in his *Theses on Feuerbach* where Marx writes: "The chief defect of all hitherto existing materialism—that of Feuerbach included, is that the thing, reality, sensuousness is conceived only in the form of an object or of *contemplation,* but not as *human sensuous activity, practice,* not subjectively. Hence it happened that the *active* side, in contradistinction to materialism, was developed by idealism—but only abstractly, since, of course, idealism does not know real, sensuous activity as such."[13]

With this discovery of the sensuous activity and practical deployment of consciousness, Marx is able to reorient the classical concept of consciousness in such a manner that it no longer simply serves the function of a theoretic-epistemological grounding of human thought. Consciousness, as it emerges in a world of work and in the social interaction of daily affairs, takes on the form of 'sentient-imbued praxis. This makes it possible to understand the development of Marx from the *Economic and Philosophic Manuscripts of 1844* to the *Theses on Feuerbach* as a fleshing out of his concept of species-being with a notion of praxis, initiating the formulation of an explicit philosophical anthropology of *praxis.*

It is at this juncture that Marx's reformulation of Feuerbach's philosophical anthropology becomes decisive. Feuerbach's approach, according to Marx, was still too heavily weighted in the direction of an abstract self-reflection. For Marx the reflexivity of self-consciousness yields not primarily consciousness as object of thought, as Feuerbach still held, but rather a praxis-imbued consciousness positioned in the midst of historical struggle and social interaction. Marxian praxis, as Merleau-Ponty has observed, cannot be subjugated to the postulate of a theoretical consciousness. "The profound philosophical meaning of the notion of praxis is to place us in an order which is not that of knowledge but rather that of communication, exchange, and association."[14] We would only recommend a modification in Merleau-Ponty's formulation of Marxian praxis so as to make explicit the *integration* of knowledge with "communication, exchange, and association." It is not that Marxian praxis is bereft of a knowledge component per se. It is rather that it provides a critique of the pure theoretical knowledge borne by an abstract self-reflexivity of consciousness.

Marx's introduction of praxis as the more inclusive frame for his anthropological reflections is of critical importance, for it is precisely this notion that provides the occasion for the merging of anthropological and ethical concerns; however, it remains questionable whether Marx himself fully succeeded in effecting such a merger. We do see, however, in these early writings of Marx a recognition of the interlacing of cognitive and ethical interests. The importance of the ethical comes to the fore in Marx's dramatic proclamation in the celebrated eleventh thesis on Feuerbach, which makes it clear that Marx is as much, if not more, concerned with the *liberation* of man as he is with the *definition* of man. Again, this does not mean that Marx has abandoned his concern to achieve an understanding of man in his socio-historical development; it means only that the Feuerbachian model of abstract self-reflexivity is no longer adequate for the task. The concept of species-being, used in the *Manuscripts* in the service of unpacking the structure of alienated labor, is refashioned so as to provide a basis for social action and a posture of redress.[15] This of course was already implicit in Marx's analysis of alienated labor and private property in his *Manuscripts,* which conclude with an appeal to an emancipation of universal humanity through the establishment of authentic communal life-relationships. Marx's notion of praxis makes this posture of redress explicit. It is this normative feature within Marx's notion of praxis that received such widespread attention in the postwar recovery of the early Marx, and inaugurated the burgeoning literature on "Marxian humanism." Viewed from this perspective, the notion of praxis functions principally as an ethical appeal to combat the alienation and eventual dehumanization which results from the production and exchange relations in capitalistic society.

Although the possibilities for a successful integration of knowledge and praxis would seem to have been present in Marx's replacement of the idealist postulate of theoretical consciousness with a concrete and praxis-oriented "human sensuous activity," it was the destiny of Marx to be appropriated and refashioned by Marxists in such a manner that these possibilities of uniting knowledge and value interest within the warp and woof of praxis were suppressed. Marxian praxis was transformed into Marxist *technē*. In the multiple expressions of Marxist philosophy (such as Leninism, Trotskyism, Stalinism, and *Pravda* Communism), one can discern an increasing technization of knowledge and an accompanying technization of value. Knowledge more and more was modeled after the instrumentality of labor-production, leading eventually to an instrumentalist reduction of reflection. Correspondingly, the normative feature of Marxian praxis became technized and was translated into a theory of instrumental value, in which specific social goals were projected as ends and specific techniques of social change and revolution were proscribed as the proper means with which to achieve the ends.

The ramifications of this Marxist technization of knowledge and value for an understanding of the human sciences were far-reaching. The Marxists became more and more disposed to emphasize the "scientific" character of Marxism, viewing it as a science of society or, even more broadly, as a science of history. Joseph Stalin summarized one such Marxist interpretation when he wrote "Marxism is the science of the laws of development of nature and society."[16] With their instrumentalist reduction of reflection, the Marxists began to look for law-like regularities in production and exchange relationships. Hence, the Marxist "science of man" gradually found its paradigm in a science of economics which itself was modeled after the law-like relationships of a "science of nature." More precisely, both the science of man and the science of nature were forced into a technological frame designed to uncover and validate the law-like relationships of socio-economic development through a species of feedback-controlled instrumental action.[17]

Another ramification of the Marxist technization of knowledge and value is the peculiar indictment, and eventual rejection, of all existing human sciences. Having transformed Marxian praxis into a technique of redress, wherewith to achieve the proposed end for humanity (freedom from class conflict) through the instrumentation of the proper means which themselves can be justified in terms of the end, Marxism was forced to indict the very existence of the current human sciences because of their fall into the ideology of class consciousness. The human sciences, according to the Marxist, simply serve the interests of the ruling class and thus are marked for abolition along with the class structure itself. This attitude toward the human sciences among the Marxist follows in the wake of their instrumentalizing the value dimension of Marxian praxis and construing it within the framework of a means-ends relationship. Marxian praxis is put into the service of a quasi-teleological ethical framework. Marx himself, we would maintain, was not committed to this move.

Merleau-Ponty displays a firmer grasp of the ethical posture of original Marxian praxis than do the Marxists when he writes: "The revolutionary project is not the result of a deliberate judgment, or the explicit positing of an end. . . . For class is a matter neither for observation nor decree; like the appointed order of the capitalistic system, like revolution, before being thought it is lived through as an obsessive presence, as possibility, enigma, and myth."[18] Admittedly, Marx himself did not work out the ethical posture of his new notion of praxis as sensuous human activity. It would seem, however, that his notion of praxis lends itself neither to a teleological nor to a deontological typology. In fact, it opens up the avenue to a radical critique of traditional value theory. Praxis is governed neither by objective ends nor by transempirical oughts. It deploys a preobjective field of concerns in which a functioning intentionality of aspirations and expectations responds to the concrete conditions of the times.

The specific ethical posture is thus one of a discernment of proper responses to existential particularities rather than the positing of objective ends or an appeal to an abstract realm of oughts. Existential responsibility replaces both teleological and deontological ethics. But in the hands of the Marxists, this original posture of Marxian praxis was distorted when it was construed as a means-end relationship and put to the service of a theory of instrumental action. Arrogating to itself a knowledge of the end of man beyond ideology, Marxism was forced to assume the stance of an indictment of the existing human sciences because of their alleged ideological residue. Because it identified all reflection with idealistic reflection, the integrity of reflection itself was threatened. Hence, Marxism soon found itself in the predicament of no longer being able to interrogate the *origin* of the human sciences through a radical reflection. It could only position itself against them.

Versions of the Marxist critique of the human sciences as

ideologically imbued have recurred in the subsequent developments within this tradition, and, interestingly enough, even in
the interpreters of Marx who see his early philosophical anthropology of praxis and ethical humanism as a passing phase in
the internal development of his thought. Such is the case with the
structuralist Marxism of Louis Althusser. According to Althusser,
in the later philosophy of Marx the earlier notion of praxis is subordinated to a scientific theory of history which is based on the
structuralist distinction between superstructure and infrastructure
and an economic determinism of production forces and exchange
relations. This shift, continues Althusser, was occasioned by a *coupure épistémologique,* occurring between 1845 and 1848, which sep-
arates Marx's early, humanistic philosophical anthropology from
his later science of history. "This rupture with every philosophical
anthropology or humanism is no secondary detail; it is Marx's scientific discovery."[19] The early thought of Marx, according to this
structuralist interpreter, is still imbued with the rhetoric of German classical philosophical ideology; and only in his later science
of history do we have a standpoint for assessing the contributions
of the human sciences. And it is precisely from this standpoint,
Althusser argues, that the human sciences fall under indictment.
Writing in his *Politics and History,* he concludes:

> The so-called Human Sciences still occupy the old continent. They
> are now armed with the latest ultra-modern techniques of
> mathematics, etc. but they are still based theoretically on the same
> outworn ideological notions as they were in the past, ingeniously
> rethought and retouched. With a few remarkable exceptions, the
> prodigious development of the so-called human sciences, above all
> the development of the social sciences, is no more than an
> *aggiornamento* of old techniques of social adaptation and social
> readaptation: of ideological techniques.[20]

When all is said and done, the human sciences, in spite of their
claims to be scientific, are found to be deceptively unscientific.
They have been unable to avoid the insinuation of ideological interests. We must point out, however, that Althusser's understanding and use of ideology is somewhat idiosyncratic within the
Marxist tradition. Ideology for Althusser is not in itself a negativity to be catalogued with the historical contingencies that will be
overcome with the dawn of scientific socialism. It is, if you will, a
positive feature in the social life of man. "So ideology is not an
aberration or contingent excrescence of History; it is a structure
essential to the historical life of societies. . . . a matter of the *lived*
relation between men and their world."[21] Althusser applies his

structuralist methodology to ideology itself and redefines it as an abiding structural feature of concrete lived experience. As such, however, it is a prescientific structure which needs to be recognized as a fact of historical life but which also needs to be rendered into an instrument of deliberate social action. As a prescientific structure of life it needs to be brought to the tribunal of a science of history and, thus, put to use in the interest of the emancipation of mankind. But it is precisely at this point that Althusser's program succumbs to some serious conceptual difficulties, chief of which is the inability to account for that reflective stance from which a science of history is able to sort out and distinguish the prejudicial and outworn ideological notions which attach to the current sciences of man from the positive appropriation of ideology in an emancipated science of history.

Our use of Althusser as an example of a structuralist reformulation of the Marxist perspective should help us define with more specificity the current problematic of philosophical anthropology as a tension between the model of praxis and the model of structure. This will make possible the localization of the problematic within the current debate between structuralism and Marxism as this debate centers around an assessment of the role of the sciences of man. Further, it will provide a fruitful point of departure for our radical anthropological critique.

The already well-known garden varieties of structuralism provide us with an alleged novel approach to the role and status of the human sciences. This novel approach has been articulated in a somewhat oracular fashion by Claude Lévi-Strauss, the oft-designated founder of structuralism, in his proclamation, "The human sciences will be structural or they will not be."[22] The unpacking of the meaning and implications of this proclamation is not an easy task, given the colorful variety of structuralisms that have been proffered by the different representatives. The meaning of structure in these varieties does not seem to be of a seamless web. The developmental approach of Piaget provides a different conceptual tapestry than does the agentic approach of Lévi-Strauss. Barthes is critical of the formalistic grammar to which both Piaget and Lévi-Strauss appeal. Lacan makes use of a psychoanalytical model of structure which is not shared by all of his intellectual compatriots. And Foucault is not sure whether he wants to be called a structuralist at all. Yet these influential men of letters have played a visible role in the formation of the *Science de l'Homme* movement that has made a notable impact upon contemporary French intellectual life in particular.[23] We are particularly interested in discerning the structuralist answer to the issue of the

unity of the sciences of man and critically assessing their rejection
of the anthropological motif as a proper philosophical framework.

When Lévi-Strauss says that the human sciences will be structural or they will not be, he seems to be telling us basically two
things: (1) classical philosophical anthropology, with its preoccupation with the human subject, no longer is adequate to the task
of grounding and unifying the human sciences; and (2) any program for the unification of the human sciences can productively
proceed only on the basis of a recognition of an invariant, synchronic infrastructure of the human mind which antedates the
phenomenal and diachronic manifestations in the life of man and
the life of society. Although there appear to be some notable
differences among the various structuralists regarding the programmatic claim in point 2, the general rejection of philosophical
anthropology expressed in point 1 seems to be more universally
accepted by the various representatives, including the neostructuralist Michel Foucault. The dissolution of the human subject is a
theme that appears and reappears throughout the structuralist literature. Indeed, it may well be designated the central motif of
structuralism. The accentuation of this motif occasioned a state of
confrontation with postwar existentialism, particularly in its
French expression, which still proceeded from the truth of the
Cartesian *cogito*. The dissolution of the human subject motif
breaks into contemporary French thought as a counter-claim to
Sartre's insistence that the "subjectivity of the individual" is the
only valid point of departure and that "there can be no other
truth to take off from than this: *I think; therefore, I exist*."[24]

The counter-claim to Sartre's existentialist thesis is most explicitly voiced by Lévi-Strauss in his book *The Savage Mind*, in
which he informs the reader that the ultimate goal of the human
sciences is "not to constitute, but to dissolve man."[25] Echoes of this
counterclaim can be heard in Foucault's thematic of the "anthropological sleep," which announces the death of man as a
sequel to Nietzsche's proclamation of the death of God. Human
subjectivity, articulated in terms of an analytic of finitude and
historicity, is for Foucault philosophically moribund. Now it is important to keep in mind that what is ultimately at stake in this
dissolution of the human subject is the elimination of *particular,
finite, historical* subjectivity. The *human mind*, we learn from Lévi-
Strauss, is spared. The finite, historical subject succumbs, but not
the human mind. Indeed, the human mind, as the underlying infrastructure, remains as the native and sole inhabitant of the sub-
terrain; and the final goal of the structural scientist is to trace the
logic of this disembodied mind in abstraction from those particu-

lar individual subjects who might happen to exemplify it. What is at issue, concludes Lévi-Strauss, is "the human mind, unconcerned with the identity of its occasional bearers."[26]

Lévi-Strauss's proposed dissolution of the human subject and the corresponding appeal to a universal and objective mind, severed from its particularized occasional bearers, provides the key to the structuralist model for the sciences of man. Structural analysis in anthropology, sociology, ethnology, psychoanalysis, political science, economics, and above all linguistics is the procedure whereby we work our way through the superficial manifestations of life, labor, and language on the superstructure level to the underlying and invariant logical grammar of oppositions and correlations, exclusions and inclusions, compatibilities and incompatibilities which constitute the infrastructure of objective mind. Thus, the special human sciences in their use of structural analysis will be in the privileged position of being able to sort out the synchronic invariables from the diachronic succession of events. It is this synchronic dimension that provides the ultimate focus of intelligibility, and it is precisely at this juncture that the antihistorical stance of structuralism becomes evident. The understanding and interpretation of concrete historical agents and actions gives way to an identification, delineation, and synthesis of abstracted structures. Lived history gives way to history as a matrix of transformations. The meanings, motives, and actions of particular men in particularized history (Lévi-Strauss's "occasional bearers" of universal mind) are understood, insofar as they are "understood" at all, from a vantage point above rather than within history. We are, therefore, not surprised to be told by Lévi-Strauss in his polemic against Sartre that we understand history only insofar as we are able to get out of it.[27] The unifying principle for the sciences of man is not to be found in the arena of interest-imbued concrete historical experience. It is localized in a transhistorical structure.

In discerning the intention and peculiar consequences of the general structuralist thesis, "the human sciences will be structural or they will not be," we see the emergence of a conflict of models in the structuralist confrontation with Marxism: structure vs. praxis. As we have indicated, Althusser sought to resolve this conflict by relegating the philosophical anthropology of praxis to the early, immature period of Marx's thought and exegeting a model of structure out of the later Marx in the form of a structural science of history. This is not the place to develop an assessment of Althusser's rather bold reinterpretation of Marx, in which, clearly, many difficulties abound. Our interest resides rather in specifying the conceptual dilemma which results from the confrontation of the structure model with the praxis model, and addressing the consequence of this dilemma for any future designs for philosophical anthropology in its effort to come to grips with the issue of the origin of the human sciences.

The structuralist model saddles us with a set of concerns quite different from those contributed by the Marxists in their appropriation and readjustment of Marxian praxis. For the Marxists, the problem is one of finding a place for the human sciences within a historical self-formative process which is infected with ideology. The human sciences, it is alleged from this perspective, have taken over, for the most part unconsciously, the ideological frame of mind and techniques that continue to permeate man's lived history, thus requiring the use of praxis as a principle of redress. The human sciences remain servants to the false consciousness permeating bourgeoise ideas and techniques. This false consciousness, according to the Marxists, needs to be purified. But it is precisely here that the problematic of the Marxist proposal becomes apparent. How does one purify a consciousness that is itself enveloped by ideology? How does consciousness step out of its condition of "falsity"? Where is the standpoint from which false consciousness and ideological perversion can be properly critiqued? The structuralist model generates problems of another sort. The structuralist seeks to establish a standpoint beyond the diachronic succession of lived history. He purports to speak from the synchronic standpoint of universal mind and its invariant grammar; or possibly the invariant grammar "speaks" through him, for the structuralist himself is but an "occasional bearer" of universal mind. Whereas the Marxist in his use of the praxis model is committed to take seriously the concrete actions and inspirations of men in history but is unable to fashion a clear idea of the human sciences because all that he sees in history is ideology; the structuralist in his use of the structure model appeals to a universal and transhistorical objective mind at the expense of the significations of lived history, which, by his own admission, must be left behind.

It could thus be said that whereas the Marxist cannot discover the idea of a human science because he doesn't know what he is looking for, the structuralist already has the idea of a human science and hence no longer needs to look. In the one case, the integrity of reflection is threatened by the absorption of thought into ideology; in the other case, the interests and passions of human agents and historical actors are sublated into a universal mind. On the one hand, we have the speech of human interest without a logos; on the other hand, we have a universal logos in the guise of an invariant grammar without the word as spoken. The one stays with the text of history and its mobile characters and loses all reflective distance; the other appeals to a transhistorical text of structural oppositions and conjunctions and abandons the concrete historical subject. The one cannot have a human science because there is no science without ideology; the other cannot have a science of that which is human because the human subject is dissolved.

How does one move beyond this dilemma? Can the requirement of praxis on the one hand and structure on the other be satisfied in such a manner that the endemic problems of Marxism and structuralism are avoided? It is the challenge of radical reflection to accomplish this task. But this task can be accomplished only through a radical interrogation of the inquiry-framework of classical philosophical anthropology and a recasting of the problem of the unity of the sciences of man into a question about origins. The fulfillment of this project will demand a critical confrontation, not only with the specific designs of Marxism and structuralism, but also with the idealist presuppositions of classical philosophical anthropology that we have traced above.

One of the questions that will need to be put to the friends of Marxism is whether their delineation of the field of praxis is not itself unduly restricted. The genius of Marx was to discern, in his understanding of praxis as "human sensuous activity," the profound limitations not only of the Cartesian substance-oriented view of consciousness but also of the idealist model of theoretical self-reflexivity which continued to inform the philosophical anthropology of Feuerbach and his successors. The praxis-oriented consciousness of human sensuous activity bursts its epistemological cocoon of theoretic-abstract consciousness and finds itself thrust into the world of practical and personal concerns. We accept this reorientation of the posture of consiousness on the part of Marx as a notable advance. Yet, in the final analysis, this new birth of praxis-oriented consciousness suffers some limitations and restrictions of its own, particularly within the later developments of Marxism. We have already intimated in our previous discussion what these might be. These intimations need now be made explicit.

Two points of radical critique need to be raised in connection with the Marxist notion of praxis. The first has to do with the persisting general tendency toward a restrictiveness of scope within the intentionality of praxis, whereby praxis is geared more and more in the direction of socio-economic interests and ethical concerns attendant to these interests. "Human sensuous activity," we submit, involves not only the praxis of concrete relations of exchange, association, and labor, but also the consciousness of my body as the concrete link between human existence and the world, the intentionality of perception, the revelatory power of the aesthetic imagination, the signification of the spoken word, the project of communication, the enjoyment of play, and the mythopoetic character of thought. All these, and more, are possible postures of human sensuous activity. It might well be said that in developing the notion of praxis, the Marxists failed to remain true to the fecundity of Marx's original insight and permitted praxis to congeal into a socio-economic matrix which restricted the possibilities of its vibrant and intentional expressiveness. This set the stage for a species of reductionism, both in the anthropological and ethical domain.

Our second criticism has to do with a more specific feature of the Marxist restriction of the significations of praxis. We have already alluded to the peculiar technization of knowledge and ethics that is at work in Marxist thought. We must now consider those features that tend to give rise to this technization. Three such features that carry a peculiar weight are: (1) the projected reduction of the science of man to a new science of nature, (2) the modeling of reflection after the pragmatics of production and technical control, and (3) the instrumentalization of value.

In its effort to become scientific, Marxism looked for a new science of nature which would do justice to the facts of man's socio-historical development. This new science of nature, according to the Marxists, can no longer be a science modeled after the mechanistic frame of traditional materialism. Such a mechanistic materialism fails to account for the dialectic of social life. What is required is a science which can incorporate the facts of socio-economic production and exchange relations so as to render them intelligible within a framework of law-like connections and "feedback" control. Such a socio-economic science of nature, it is alleged, will make room for an understanding of man in a way which is quite different from the "naturalisms" of traditional thought. This transfigured meaning of the science of nature, which makes possible the incorporation of a science of man within it, can then be seen to correspond with a notion of reflection which is itself modeled after the interests and designs of production and technical control. Knowledge is brought into close association with the orientations of interest within praxis, but these orientations of interest are ultimately subordinated to the pragmatics of production and instrumental action in which praxis is construed principally as a matter of technique and social control.

It is at this point that the portrait of "economic man," with its calculation and engineering of satisfactions and dissatisfactions, begins to surface.

The instrumentalization of value follows closely on the heels of this technization of practical knowledge. In the movement from the technized cognitive interests within the project of an under-standing of man to the ethical interest in the program for the emancipation of man, a continuing accent on instrumentality exists. This means that in the ethical domain reflection becomes an instrument of redress and social engineering, and values be-come the instrumental means for achieving socially desirable ends. The implicit "theory of value" that continues to inform Marxist thought is thus based on a paradigm of instrumental action which legislates a means-ends framework of analysis.

It is at this juncture that the Marxist conception of reflection and science along the lines of the model of production and its ethical program of redress and social transformation coalesce. Praxis is understood as that instrumental reflection and action in which the world of nature is appropriated through the implemen-tation of a socio-economic science that provides for an eman-cipation of man by the technical control of social labor. This socio-economic science is ultimately identified with natural science in that it proceeds by dint of the discernment of law-like relation-ships and calculated control. Praxis is thus restricted to the inter-est of a technical control of satisfactions and an economy of profitable decisions that will ensure emancipation from the alienation of necessary labor.

We must, therefore, conclude that the Marxist praxis model with its restricting sedimentation of the field of consciousness, its technizing of reflection, and its instrumentalizing of value pro-vides neither an adequate horizon for the project of self-understanding nor a viable frame of inquiry for the pursuit of the question of the origin of the sciences of man. As we have seen, it results, particularly in its ethical expression, in the congealing of praxis as a principle of redress wherewith the human sciences can only be indicted because of their ideological content. This praxis, furthermore, is so imbued with technique-oriented interests that the result is a virtual abandonment of the resources of reflection which might account for the integrity of thought. An ideological impasse blocks the path to a self-understanding beyond the pale of false consciousness. A broader notion of praxis and a richer concept of reflection is required to proceed beyond this impasse.

However, recourse to the structure model of contemporary structuralism at this juncture provides little solace. Although the structuralist critique of subjectivity is something from which one can learn much, in the end the structuralist, as we have seen, subordinates the diachrony of praxis to a synchrony of modal transformations and loses not only the existing subject but history itself. Seeking a standpoint outside of history, the structuralist sacrifices the significations of the speech acts of communicative discourse and the multivalence of concrete bodily, perceptual, and aesthetic world-experience, not because of an unwarranted restriction built into the field of praxis, as is the case in Marxism, but because of a superimposition of structure. This structure translates the concrete significations of the events of speech and consciousness into a logic of universal mind modeled after linguistic science.[28] System and structure take precedence over event and praxis, and classification in the form of a logic of oppositions takes precedence over historical self-understanding. In such a scheme of things, the question of the archaeology of knowledge and the origin of the sciences of man must remain forever misplaced. The *archē*, as discussed particularly by Foucault, is located on the hither side of history after the "death of man" has come to full realization. But such a localization of the *archē* leads ultimately to an occlusion rather than to a disclosure of the origin of the sciences of man. If Lévi-Strauss's dictum, "The human sciences will be structural or they will not be," would indeed provide us with a forced option, we would have to conclude that they will not be.

In this chapter we have traced certain aspects of the development of philosophical anthropology from the anthropological reflections of Kant and Hegel to the contemporary problematic of the conflict of praxis and structure in the designs of Marxism and structuralism. We have noted the unavoidable impact that the developing special human sciences have had on the definition of the province of philosophical anthropology, and we have delineated the impasse that this confrontation has occasioned within the inquiry frameworks of Marxism and structuralism. The way out of this impasse, we maintain, is not via a displacement of the anthropological question, as structuralsim would have us believe. Rather, the way out is via a radicalization of anthropological reflection, which at the same time marks out a new terrain for explorations into self and historical understanding and a fresh approach to the question concerning the origin of the sciences of man. In the next chapters, we will articulate the form that such radical anthropological reflection takes.

NOTES

1. *Anthropologie in pragmatischer Hinsicht, Kant's Werke,* Band VII (Berlin: Georg Reimer, 1917). This work contains various lectures that Kant gave on the subject between 1772 and 1797.

2. *Kant's Introduction to Logic,* trans T. K. Abbott (New York: Philosophical Library, 1963), p. 15.

3. *Ibid.*

4. A comprehensive and illuminating discussion of the importance of philosophical anthropology for Kant's philosophy as a whole is provided by Frederick P. Van de Pitte in his book, *Kant as Philosophical Anthropologist* (The Hague: Martinus Nijhoff, 1971).

5. *The Encyclopedia of Philosophy,* Vol. 6, ed. Paul Edwards (New York: Macmillan, 1967), p. 160.

6. *Fischer-Lexicon: Philosophie,* eds. Diemer and Frensel (Fischer Verlag: Frankfurt-Main, 1958), pp. 18, 20.

7. For a helpful discussion of the development and representatives of these subdisciplines in philosophical anthropology see the above referenced essay by H. O. Pappé in *The Encyclopedia of Philosophy,* pp. 159–66.

8. Paul Ricoeur addresses this issue in his perceptive article "The Antinomy of Human Reality and the Problem of Philosophical Anthropology," when he writes: "On the 'theoretical' level, the only mediation is external; it is the *thing*: the unity of understanding and sensibility, which Kant called the transcendental imagination, is only a condition for the possibility of the synthesis in the object; the unity of happiness and character is a *task:* and this task is what we call the idea of the person. The synthesis of understanding and sensibility is not 'for itself' because it is the project of an object; the synthesis of happiness and character has *to become for itself,* since it is the project of the person." *Readings in Existential Phenomenology,* eds. N. M. Lawrence and D. O'Conner (Englewood Cliffs: Prentice-Hall, 1967), p. 398.

9. *The Philosophy of History,* trans. J. Sibree (New York: Dover Publications, 1956), p. 17.

10. Manfred H. Vogel provides this characterization of Feuerbach in his "Introduction" to his translation of *Principles of the Philosophy of the Future* (Indianapolis: Bobbs-Merrill, 1966), p. viii.

11. *The Essence of Christianity,* trans. George Eliot (New York: Harper & Brothers, 1957, pp. 1, 2.

12. *Economic and Philosophic Manuscripts,* trans. T. B. Bottomore; in Erich Fromm, *Marx's Concept of Man* (New York: Frederick Ungar, 1961), p. 101.

13. *The Marx-Engels Reader,* ed. Robert C. Tucker (New York: W. W. Norton, 1972), p. 107.

14. *The Adventures of the Dialectic,* trans. J. Bien (Evanston: Northwestern University Press, 1973), p. 50.

15. For an extended discussion of this point see Klaus Hartmann, "Praxis: A Ground for Social Theory?", *Journal of the British Society for Phenomenology,* Vol, 1, No. 2, 1970, p. 48.

16. *Marxism and Linguistics* (New York: International Publishers, 1951), p. 47.

17. We are in fundamental agreement with Habermas's claim that Marxism blurred the distinction between praxis and *technē* and thus restricted the knowledge component of praxis-imbued interest. However, we remain critical of Habermas's failure to distinguish clearly enough Marxian from Marxist praxis. It would appear that it is only in the latter that the reduction of reflection to the model of production and the sublation of the science of man into an instrumental science of nature is achieved. We are particularly critical of his use of Marx's well-known, programmatic statement in the *Manuscripts* — "Natural science will eventually subsume the science of man just as the science of man will subsume natural science: there will be a *single* science" — as a basis for the claim that Marx himself effected a quasi-positivist reduction of the human sciences to a natural science of economic law-like relations. After quoting the above from the *Manuscripts,* Habermas concludes: "This demand for a natural science of man, with its positivist overtones, is astonishing" (*Knowledge and Human Interests,* p. 46). What we find "astonishing" is rather that Habermas has seen fit to take the first part of the quotation from Marx as the substance of Marx's thought, neglecting the second part in which Marx sees natural science as being "subsumed" under the science of man. Admittedly, what Marx might mean by a "single science" in this instance is not at all clear, but to exegete the meaning of the passage in such a manner that it becomes a statement of a positivist reduction of human science to natural science is surely to put an undue strain on the text.

18. *Phenomenology of Perception,* trans. Colin Smith (New York: The Humanities Press, 1962), pp. 445, 446.

19. *For Marx,* trans. Ben Brewster (New York: Pantheon, 1969), p. 227.

20. *Politics and History,* trans. Ben Brewster (London: NLB, 1972), p. 167.

21. *For Marx,* pp. 232, 233.

22. Quoted in Howard Gardner, *The Quest for Mind* (New York: Random House, 1972), p. 246.

23. A wide spectrum of writings by some of the representatives of French structuralism has been made available to the English-speaking world by Richard Macksey and Eugenio Donato in their edited volume, *The Languages of Criticism and the Sciences of Man: The Structuralist Controversy* (Baltimore: Johns Hopkins Press, 1970).

24. *Existentialism and Human Emotions* (New York: Philosophical Library, 1957), p. 36.

25. *The Savage Mind* (Chicago: University of Chicago Press, 1966), p. 247.

26. "Overture to *le Cru et le cuit*," trans. J. H. McMahon; in *Structuralism,* ed. Jacques Ehrmann (New York: Doubleday, 1970), p. 49.

27. *The Savage Mind,* p. 262.

28. See particularly Lévi-Strauss, *Structural Anthropology,* Part I: "Language and Kinship," trans. C. Jacobson and B. G. Schoepf (New York: Doubleday, 1967).

CHAPTER 3

The Radicalization of Knowledge

The movement beyond philosophical anthropology by way of radical anthropological reflection results in a relocation of standpoint of questioning. From this new standpoint of questioning, we are able critically to address the informing presuppositions and programmatic claims of traditional philosophical anthropology that have been sketched in the preceding chapter. There is a need, first of all, for a critique of the concept of philosophical foundations. Such a critique, it is hoped, will reestablish the relevance of prephilosophical and prescientific comprehension for philosophy and the human sciences alike. Secondly, the new standpoint of questioning in radical anthropological reflection opens the possibility for a critique of the primacy of the principle of self-reflexive consciousness, a principle that has directed and informed the traditional search for rational, apodictic foundations. Thirdly, with this shift of standpoint, radical anthropology will be in position to transpose the question of the *unity of the sciences* into a question about the *origin of the sciences*. We will thus see how the loss of center, which is of such concern to philosophical anthropology in its confrontation with the diversification of the special human sciences, is rectified not by an integration and unification of the methodologies and codified results of the special sciences, but rather by a recovery of the originative matrix or setting in which thought and action are postured.

The foundation metaphor, which has been with us for some time now, has frequently been employed by philosophers to illustrate the need for an Archimedean point in the realm of ideas at which to secure judgments and insights relative to both knowledge and value. Epistemology and ethics alike have been defined in terms of the requirement for a durable foundation which will yield an unimpeachable ground for a theory of judgment on the one hand and a theory of value on the other. The tradition has time and again proclaimed the ideals of pure theory and philosophical rationality as undisputable axioms for inquiries into knowledge and value. Knowledge without a theoretical foundation, which anchors the various judgmental acts and accounts for the validation of their contents, would within such a scheme of analysis hardly be knowledge at all. Correspondingly, values without a stable criteria of justification would lose their obliging character. Thus we see in the time-honored disciplines of epistemology and axiology the requirement for a pure, theoretical, philosophical grounding. This requirement is seen to apply not only to the project of philosophical analysis itself, but also to the task of comprehending the nature of the special sciences and coordinating their varied results. This confers upon philosophical reason a staggering responsibility. Not only must it garner the foundations for its own operations, it must also incorporate the projects of the special sciences, physical and social, into its citadel of pure theory. This results in what we might call the "Greyhound syndrome" in the stance of the philosopher as he confronts the scientist: "Leave the thinking to us!" It is this *hybris* of philosophical reason and pure theory, used in the interests of securing a fundamental grounding, that radical anthropological reflection in its radicalization of knowledge and value brings under critique. Its aim is to bring to view a world of prephilosophical and prescientific comprehension which antedates the theoretical constructs of pure theory. This prephilosophical and prescientific comprehension functions within the context of an expanded form of reason and a more concrete reflection, not yet framed by the dichotomies of theory and practice, the logical and the empirical, fact and value. Thus it would be proper to characterize radical anthropological reflection, in its movement beyond philosophical anthropology, as a type of *protophilosophy*.

A long-standing tradition in Western philosophy has been that one of the principal goals of philosophical reflection is to establish secure epistemological and metaphysical foundations. Philosophical anthropology in its development as a special philosophical discipline was unable to resist the lure of this time-honored goal. Drawing from the tradition of transcendental idealism out of which it developed, it designed an anthropology of knowledge in which the idealist principle of self-reflexive consciousness continued to inform its inquiry standpoint. This principle, if judiciously employed, was to lead to the promised land of unassailable foundations. Knowledge was grounded in an epistemological subject whose distinguishing feature was consciousness—consciousness of objects and principally consciousness of itself as subject of consciousness. Thus the foundations were solidified through a species of epistemic self-reflexivity, entrusted with the task of perpetually retrieving the contents of subjectivity. Admittedly, in its early Marxian and existentialist expression philosophical anthropology was able to liberate itself from a narrow theoretical self-reflexivity of pure thought and recognize the contributions of praxis and existential passion. Yet, neither the early Marx nor the existentialists were entirely successful in surmounting the idealist model of self-reflexivity and the lure of subjectivity. Radical anthropological reflection is geared to a radicalization of the movement of self-reflexivity so as to overcome its premise of subjectivity as a philosophical principle. Existentialism surmounted the prejudices and falsifications of the cult of objectivity; radical anthropology proceeds one step further and counters the subjectivity that continues to inform the model of self-reflexive consciousness. The radicalized reflexivity of radical anthropology will take the form of a reflexivity upon an originary matrix of thought and action in which neither subjectivity nor objectivity has yet established residency. It will be a reflexivity upon originative experience rather than a self-reflexivity of an epistemological subject.

In searching for the foundations of knowledge of man in the domain of subjectivity, philosophical anthropology was forced to assume the extraordinarily difficult task of coordinating and integrating the objectifying procedures and results of the rapidly developing special sciences of man within a perspective of subjectivity and self-reflexive consciousness. Not only did this task assume responsibilities that were enormous, it proceeded from a questionable framework of interrogation. Just as positivism was unable to achieve a unification of the sciences from the standpoint of objectivity (logic and semantics) because every effort at objectifying consciousness foundered, so philosophical anthropology failed to achieve its projected integration of the human sciences by proceeding from the domain of consciousness and subjectivity. Ironically, the root error in positivism and philosophical anthropology, relative to their attitudes toward the special sciences, was the same. The unification of the sciences of man became a philosophical problem and task (methodological critique for positivism and exploration of the structure of subjectivity for philosophical anthropology) of somehow integrating the already objectified procedures and results of the special sciences. But this general definition of the problem is precisely what requires critical scrutiny.

Radical anthropological reflection no longer approaches the issue as a problem of unifying the methodological procedures of the various sciences nor one of coordinating and integrating their codified results. The problem becomes an interrogation of the origin of scientific and philosophical analysis and construction alike, as this analysis and construction take their rise from the matrix of an originary encounter with the world in its variegated presentment. The unification envisaged by classical philosophical anthropology is something that would occur *after* the results of technical theory construction and the codified empirical findings were delivered; the quest for an origin interrogates the texture of world experience *before* the constructionism of theory and the codification of empirical facts. Admittedly, already instituted theories and definitions of fact color the fabric of experience at every given point in its history, but this does not displace the requirement for a reclamation of that originary experience from which *theoria* first emerges and to which it must return time and again to insure its relevance.

The protophilosophical and protoscientific character of radical anthropology, as it has been summarily sketched above, implies in a singularly profound sense a radicalization of knowledge and value. It is ultimately through such a radicalization that the metaphysico-epistemological and axiological constructions that have informed the reflection on man in traditional philosophical anthropology can be dismantled and assessed. Considerations pertaining to knowledge and value have, of course, been pretty much at the philosophical center of things from the time of the Greeks; but they have elicited a particular fascination for the modern philosophers, and they have been central in the recent attempts to understand and cope with the crisis in the human sciences. These considerations have been uppermost in the current preoccupation with questions about the nature of scientific inquiry, rules of inference, canons of verification, the possibility of a value-free science, the "ought" and the "is," and many more. Our present concern, however, is not to address the very general and amorphous fields of knowledge and value theory as such, but rather to isolate certain features of the general issues which pertain to the question of man's knowledge of himself. This question has a clear and discernible Socratic ring to it. Regrettably, however, the accelerated developments in the current sciences of man not only make a Socratic answer to it enormously difficult, but they also have tended to suppress any trenchant examination of the nature of the question that is being asked.

Admittedly, there is a sense in which Kant's question, "What is man?" and the primacy which he ascribed to it in his *Introduction to Logic*, provide the touchstone for our program of radical anthropology. However, this question needs to be asked in such a manner that it no longer marks out the path to a philosophical concept of human nature or a transcendental unification of the faculties of human knowledge and action. The question needs to be reformulated so as to become a question about man's understanding and interpretation of himself within the fabric of his originary, lived experience rather than a question about a possible philosophical concept of "human nature." The political theorist Fred R. Dallmayr helps direct us to the proper path when he writes: "The task of a humanism in our time cannot simply be to resurrect a compact and apodictic model of 'human nature'— divorced from empirical findings and concrete experience. The proliferation of information suggests a more modest aim: to explore and delineate patiently the elusive contours of man in the midst of cultural diversity."[1] We must make clear, however, that the "empirical findings," alluded to by Professor Dallmayr, themselves require a radical investigation as to their origin. We simply cannot take for granted that the question of what comprises empirical fact has already been answered. Indeed, we will attempt to show that the empiricist-postivistic definition of fact, so uncritically taken over by many researchers in the human sciences, remains truncated and partial and is of little help precisely at that crucial point where the question about the origin of the sciences of man is raised.

Of central importance in our radicalization of the traditional project of securing a "nature" or "essence" of man is the recognition of the bearing of the socio-historical upon the phenomenon of self-understanding. The matrix of originary experience has an indelible socio-historical cast. Hence, that which is interrogated in a search for the origin is itself social and historical and resists any reduction either to a material or formal determination of a "nature." Yet, we must proceed with some caution here. We need only be reminded of the intermittent distortions of a historicism which, in its reaction to naturalism, reified "history" and proposed to understand nature through historical categories. This ushered in a veritable crisis of conceptualization in which contending parties would debate the merits of a history of human nature on the one hand and a nature of historical man on the other. The reified concepts of history and nature have for the most part contributed little to an understanding of man's originary experience.

Clearly there is a socio-historical horizon to lived experience, but there also is a physico-natural horizon. Man can neither be lifted out of history nor out of nature. The task is to elucidate these horizons in such a manner that their precategorial significations come to the fore. Merleau-Ponty has made a notable advance in the direction of a preobjective comprehension of nature and history with his notion of the lived-body as the center of the perceptual world. The lived-body is neither historical nor natural in the categorial sense. It is the base of operations and the center of concernful projects which envelop at the same time a sense of *lived through* history and a *concrete experience* of nature in every perceptual act, accomplishment of speech, and projection of a task.

Also, in the philosophical biologies of Arnold Gehlen and Helmut Plessner, we discern an awareness of the need to overcome the categorial split between nature and history. The significance of Gehlen's and Plessner's investigations is that they have called our attention to the limitations of traditional philosophical anthropology arising out of its idealistic orientation toward a self-reflexive consciousness which eventually historicizes man and deprives him of the experience of nature. A movement away from the idealistic closure of consciousness and subjectivity is particularly evident in Gehlen's accentuation of the complimentariness of man's biological heritage and his institutionalized condition, and in Plessner's elucidation of the posture of man's "eccentric position." Man's eccentric position places him in a position of contact not only with his socio-historical setting but with his biological environment as well. Man is viewed as a creature within the interstices of nature and culture, whose bodily comportment is at the same time taken over from his biological milieu and his intentionality of behavior as an expression of meaning.[2] It is interesting to note the contrast between Gehlen's and Plessner's versions of philosophical anthropology and that of Scheler. Scheler remains much more idealistically oriented. In the thought of Scheler, the hierarchy of nature-mind-spirit remains intact and his idiosyncratic redefinition of intuition simply takes over the traditional idealist function of reason as a grasping of the "essence" of spirit.

The radicalization of knowledge, wherewith the origin of philosophical analysis and the scientific study of man are to be made visible, thus proceeds from a radical critique of the ideal of a human nature which has guided traditional inquiries into the being and behavior of man. This radical critique requires a reappraisal of the timeworn institutionalized dichotomies of nature and history, the empirical and the transcendental, fact and value—all of which have continued to inform the program and designs of classical philosophical anthropology. We will set this radical critique of knowledge in motion by entering into a critical dialogue with some of the representatives of critical theory, structuralism, and phenomenology as they address the problems of the knowledge of man and the role of the human sciences.

It is in the Marxian anthropology of knowledge and in the subsequent developments of critical theory, particularly as represented in the writings of Habermas, that the issue of knowledge and value pertinent to man's understanding of himself within his socio-historical formation process has received what may be its decisive contemporary expression. We have already seen how Marx incorporated both knowledge and value interests into his philosophical anthropology, the conceptual pivots for which were supplied by Feuerbach's philosophy of man. We found that coupled with Marx's intent to comprehend man in terms of his nature-bound species-being there was a corresponding interest in the liberation of man. These two features comprise his notion of praxis. Epistemological and ethical interest are thus seen to merge. Knowledge in some way remains intertwined with value. But the manner in which knowledge is to be related to value was exactly what Marx's analysis did not make clear. There is a sense in which Marx bequeathed to his successors the requirement to rethink this issue anew. One of the more impressive responses to this bequest is discernible in the critical theory of Jürgen Habermas, particularly as formulated in *Knowledge and Human Interests*.

Habermas proposes a critical philosophical anthropology of knowledge that follows the path of self-reflection. His goal is to furnish a transcendental framework of inquiry which will make possible the explanation of the interconnection of cognition and interest. He sections out the domain of interests into technical, practical (having to do principally with communication), and emancipatory. Marx, according to Habermas, correctly discerned the inseparability of cognition and technical interest in man's self-formative socio-historical process, but the Marxists erred in their reduction of all interest to technical interest and in their paradigmatic use of the methods of natural science. Dilthey is important for Habermas because of his sensitivity to the formative effects of practical interests at work in the communicative act. In fashioning a hermeneutic for the recovery of lived meanings in the practical project of the communicative act, Dilthey pioneered the incorporation of methodical self-reflection into the social sciences and moved beyond the limitations of the natural science model still employed by the Marxists. Nonetheless, according to Habermas, in his use of biography as a model for hermeneutical understanding, Dilthey was unable to take into account the significations of the unconscious which are also essential ingredients of the self-formative process. Dilthey's heremeneutic is designed only for a reading of the text of consciousness and the surface meanings delivered up through manifest memory. What is required as a corrective to Dilthey's method, continues Habermas, is a psychoanalytical critique of meaning which provides a "depth hermeneutic" through which the distinctive relevance of emancipatory interests in man's personal and social existence can be disclosed. Psychoanalysis provides us with a self-reflection that unifies knowledge and interest in the drive for emancipation from repressive norms. Hence, the linkage of critical theory with psychoanalysis provides a scientific framework that is able to incorporate methodical self-reflection in a way in which neither the natural sciences nor the social sciences by themselves are able to do.

Habermas thus recommends a new point of departure and a new method for self-reflection. Yet this point of departure and methodological framework of inquiry remain admittedly transcendental. Hence, there is a search for a priori anthropological invariables which might enjoy a priority over the contingent historical events in man's self-formation process. From this standpoint Habermas is able to address the issue of the grounding of the human sciences. The human sciences are seen to have their foundation in the methodical self-reflection of a critical-transcendental anthropology. Not only is the foundation-metaphor at work here, pointed in the direction of a philosophical grounding, this philosophical grounding assumes the character of *veritas transcendentalis*.

Admittedly, Habermas is aware that classical transcendental philosophy lacks the requisite resources to reintegrate theory and practice, knowledge and interest; yet he fashions his framework of analysis in such a manner that the distinctions between the transcendental and the empirical, the a priori and the experiential, the necessary and the contingent, remain intact. When issues of theory and cognition are under discussion, there is an appeal to transcendental analysis with its promise of a priori necessity and universality; when issues of practice and interest are under discussion, there is recourse to empirical analysis in recognition of the variability of contingent, historical fact. But theory and practice, knowledge and interest, are allegedly to be understood as being of one piece; hence transcendental analysis must somehow penetrate the contingency of the empirical, and empirical analysis must already in some sense be transcendental. In the end we are not clear where the transcendental begins and the empirical leaves off. The two domains are blended in such a manner that the empirical becomes quasi-transcendental and the transcendental quasi-empirical. The transcendental and the empirical mix and mingle in such a fashion that the contributions of each remain undefined.[3]

The path out of this quandary, we suggest, is not that of further revising and defining the character of transcendental and empirical analysis so as to make them compatible within a transcendental framework of cognitive interests, but rather that of a radical critique of the acceptance of the distinction as mandatory and foundational. Indeed, we suggest that the ascription of primacy to the transcendental-empirical distinction is precisely the reef on which any transcendental philosophical anthropology founders. A more originative notion of reflection and a more originative notion of fact than those installed by the transcendental-empirical dichotomy are required.

At this juncture it might seem that the neostructuralism of Mikel Foucault offers some promise of deliverance from the dilemma of transcendental philosophical anthropology. In *The Order of Things,* Foucault defines his project as a deconstruction of the "transcendental-empirical doublet."[4] He attempts to deconstruct this doublet by way of a sustained critique of that subjectivity which has informed the history of philosophical anthropology. If both the transcendental subject and the empirical subject are dissolved, the epistemic spaces which define the transcendental and the empirical are displaced, and a new *epistēmē* is allowed to appear. This new *epistēmē* emerges after the "death of man" and appears in the guise of the "being of language." So runs the argument in *The Order of Things.* Foucault's assessment of the problem, we submit, may be more perceptive than his proposed solution. His critique of the primacy of the subject, which he shares with many other structuralists, is insightful.

It needs to be pointed out, however, that this assessment and critique of subjectivity, transcendental as well as psychological, is hardly a "discovery" of structuralism. As early as 1947 in his *Letter on Humanism,* Heidegger made explicit the requirement to proceed beyond a humanism that is based on subjectivity or even a philosophy of man in any traditional sense. Also the later Heidegger shows a concern with language, as is the case with Foucault and the structuralists. But unlike the structuralists, Heidegger does not pursue the question of language *linguistically.* According to Heidegger, the issue of language is not a problem of linguistics, or even metalinguistics, which still remain within the framework of calculative and controlling knowledge.[5] Now it is precisely this linguistic framework which remains intact in structuralist analysis—even in the more seminal and revolutionary investigations of Foucault.

The undergrinding philosophical matrix of this linguistic framework, which was already supplied by de Saussure in his

celebrated and influential *Cours de linguistique générale,* is the distinction between synchrony and diachrony. Indeed, in effect, in
structuralist analysis the synchrony-diachrony doublet replaces the
transcendental-empirical doublet. But instead of constituting an
advance, this replacement represents a retrogression, for through
its employment the sciences of man are removed even farther
from their locus of origin. The transcendental, at least as redefined in the later philosophy of Husserl and the transcendental
anthropology of critical theory, still retains a tenuous, although
troublesome, connection with history. The synchronic, on the
other hand, severs all ties with the concrete events of lived history.
The sought after *archē,* which Foucault and the structuralists so
diligently pursue, is positioned outside of time in a nonhistorical
being of language.

Contra structuralism and its multiple garden varieties, it is our
argument that the origin of scientific and philosophical knowledge
of man is to be found *diesseits* rather than *jenseits* the world of lived
experience. Hence, a phenomenology of the life-world, such as
articulated in the later writings of Edmund Husserl, brings us
closer to the region of origin. Phenomenology does not simply
displace subjectivity, à la the "death of man" theme of structuralism; it launches a disciplined inquiry into the genealogy of
subjectivity and objectivity alike, as they emerge from a precategorial life-world. And already in phenomenology, particularly
in its third-generation expression in the thought of Merleau-Ponty
and Alfred Schutz, we discern a move beyond both the formalism
of a transcendental ego and the idiosyncratic historicity of a personal subject to the socio-historical formative context which encompass human thought and action. This, however, is not a move
which dissolves man; it contextulizes him within a broader natural
and socio-historical world. These later developments in
phenomenological philosophy provide at least a provisional
thread of Ariadne to lead us out of the perplexing labyrinth in
which both the current human sciences and formal philosophy
find themselves. Phenomenology, and more specifically a
phenomenology of human existence or "existential phenomenology," as it is commonly called, has marked out a region and path
for a sustained inquiry into the topic of a possible origin of self
and social knowledge. Yet, our project of radical anthropological
reflection requires that phenomenology itself be subjected to a
radical critique, so as to keep it from solidifying into a programmatic of pure theory.

Such a radicalization and perpetual renewal will no longer
permit the treatment of the life-world as a phenomenological re-

siduum, remaining as the permanent deposit in the wake of the
well-known transcendental-phenomenological reduction. The
transcendental framework of inquiry, even in its phenomenological modification, needs to be thought through and gone beyond.
The intrusion of lived history and the precategorial disclosure of
nature, at that point of intersection where the personal, the social,
and the environmental meet, requires a shift of standpoint. This
new standpoint, the standpoint of radical anthropology, renders
possible an interrogation of the genesis of meaning in the concrete life-world as it proceeds from a matrix of prephilosophical
and prescientific reflection. The point that requires emphasis is
that there is a genesis and development of meaning *already at work*
in the life-world. A tendency has recurred in the phenomenological literature to relegate the life-world to a prereflective and pre-
cognitive domain. As a phenomenological residuum, delivered
through the efforts of a philosophical-transcendental reflection,
the life-world is often viewed as a disorganized sequence of vis-
ceral and psychological responses to everything in general, which
must then wait upon the penetrating light of philosophical reason
to achieve order, structure, and sense. But herein we discern a
prejudiced privilege conferred upon philosophical reflection.
What is overlooked in such a scheme of things is the various forms
of insight and signification that are already operative within the
texture and flow of originary experience. These significations are
admittedly prephilosophical and prescientific but not, therefore,
devoid of knowledge-bearing comprehension. In the performance
of everyday speech, in the production and use of tools and utensils, in the handshake and in the embrace, in laughing and crying,
in the poetics of the dance, in the rituals of etiquette and religion,
in the planning of affairs of households and economy, and in the
posture of silence, a comprehension of self and world is already at
work.

The radicalization of knowledge thus leads us back to a
primordial world of prephilosophical and prescientific comprehension. The categorial thinking of philosophy and the calculative thinking of science, although not denied as legitimate
projects, are denied absolute sovereignty over the domain of
knowledge. In our search for an origin, we are led to an understanding and a comprehension that precedes the objectification
and formalization of scientific and philosophical reason. This
places us into an originary milieu of lived experience that antedates the epistemic bifurcations of the transcendental vs. the empirical, the necessary vs. the contingent, nature vs. history, and
fact vs. value. William James, that genius of attentive observation

and concrete description of human behavior and action, already
pointed us in the direction of our quest for an origin with his
"radical empiricism" and its summons to return to a "world of
pure experience."[6] Disenchanted with traditional empiricism, with
its pulverization of experience into discrete, atomistic units, and
its imported reifying abstractions, James discovered through his
radical empiricism of world experience an experiential field,
richly endowed with meaning-laden motivations, memories, anticipations, and configurations of existential moods. This experiential field, according to James, was already informed by
intentional vectors and knowledge-producing connections and
conjunctions and, hence, did not have to wait upon a transcendental ego to swoop down from on high to sort out and bind
up experience according to categorial requirements. Our search
for the origin of the human sciences receives continued inspira-
tion from the seminal investigation of James, who himself was a
psychologist of considerable acuity and perception.

The relevance of the recovery of an originary world of sense-
imbued experience for the tasks and goals of the special human
sciences was already perceived by James. Precisely within the
world of pure experience, that James so suggestively adumbrated
in his philosophical reflections, resides the origin of the human
sciences. Although James was more specifically interested in relating the discipline of psychology to his new view of experience, he
opened up the possibility of a fresh approach to the role of the
sciences of man more generally. The complex of interests, motivations, and meaning-endowed actions which comprise the world
of pure experience is ultimately the base of operations not only
for the psychological sciences but also for sociology, anthropology,
history, jurisprudence, politics, and economics. Also, we might
add, it is the base of operations for those special investigative procedures which constitute the sciences of nature, as Husserl has so
perceptively shown in his phenomenology of the life-world. As we
have repeatedly emphasized, the distinction between the domain
of nature and the domain of the socio-historical has not yet congealed into an entitive status within the flow of experience that
vitalizes the life-world. It is to this originary stream of experience
that the special sciences—natural as well as human—need perpetually to return if they are to avoid the fates of abstractionism,
formalism, and objectivism.

Alfred Schutz has penetratingly spoken to the issue at hand in
his analysis of concept-formation and theory-construction within
the social sciences. "In social science," says Schutz, "there must be
constant recourse to pregiven knowledge of the social world and

of the world in general.["7] Only by recourse to this pregiven knowledge and taken-for-granted meanings already extant in the lived social world is the social scientist able to avoid the reification of his concepts and theories as generative principles. Thus, the task of the social sciences, according to Schutz, is "to describe the processes of meaning-establishment and meaning-interpretation as these are carried out by the individuals living in the social world."[8] These are the very processes of "meaning-establishment" and "meaning-interpretation," referenced by Schutz, that we wish to emphasize in our notion of the originary matrix of experience. The human sciences as well as the philosophical study of man have their origin neither in a purified region of abstract conceptualization nor in an inchoate, disarrayed succession of sensory facts. Constellations of sense and significance are already established and already understood in the workaday world of practical projects and everyday discourse. The *logos* is already at work in lived experience.

Proceeding from the taken-for-granted shared meanings and activities within the originary stream of experience, the special sciences of man adjust their lenses to focus on particular constellations of these lived meanings. Hence, some principles and procedures for selection are required by the special human sciences. This selection should not be regarded pejoratively. As we have argued in an earlier chapter, the crisis of the human sciences cannot be attributed to the use of selective procedures. Selection is not in itself a mark of distortion or falsification. Selection is simply an implication of the finitude of human knowledge. The social scientist is required to select for investigation certain configurations of lived experience and exclude others. He sketches, if you will, a partitive profile of the life-world and classifies, organizes, and interprets the relevant data within this profile through his established investigative procedures. The selected profile may be that of meaning-imbued activities of man within the framework of his varied social institutions and cultural patterns and roles; it may be that of meaning-establishment at work in man's concern with political organization; it may be the region of an economic calculus of man's satisfactions and dissatisfactions; it may be a profile of the life-world in its constellation of playful activities and concerns; it may be the configuration of significances which attach to man as an animal who speaks; it may be a protrait of man as seen through the formative influences of his religious traditions and ecclesiastical institutions; it may be a perspective on man from the vantage point of his personal attitudes, personality traits, compulsions, and obsessions. Thus the varied portraits of *"homo sociologicus," "homo politicus," "homo oeconomicus," "homo ludens," "homo loquens," "homo ecclesiasticus,"* and "psychological man" are born. The conceptual constructs which define and designate these portraits possess a methodological legitimacy so long as their reflexive character, which preserves a liaison with the originary stream of experience, is acknowledged. Their adequacy is to be judged in terms of the degree to which they disclose and make manifest their point of origin.

Appealing to the suggestiveness and seminal disclosures in James's articulation of "the world of pure experience" and Husserl's articulation of the "life-world," we are able to move toward the origin of scientific explanation and philosophical reflection as it pertains to the question of the behavior and being of man. Proceeding from such a cognitive attitude, it could be said that the required task of each of the special human sciences is that of a special *constitution* of world. Specified worlds, and subworlds within these special worlds, are constituted out of a primordial world of originary experience.

How does such a special "constitution of world" within the various scientific and philosophical studies of man proceed? What is the meaning of "constitution" and what is the meaning of "world"? Given the somewhat standardized meaning of constitution in transcendental phenomenology, it is mandatory that we clarify our pretranscendental understanding of this operation and distinguish it from the egologically grounded constitution of transcendental phenomenology. Admittedly, the question "Who (or what) does the constituting?" would seem to be implied in any talk of world constitution. However, the answering of this question necessitates neither an appeal to a transcendental ego nor to an abstract empirical subject. Rather, we would recommend that constitution be understood as the shared project of a community of investigators and interpreters, guided by an interest in the communication of common knowledge concerns. Whether one of these common knowledge concerns involves the possible utility of the conceptual furniture of a "transcendental ego" and an "empirical subject" is not yet decided at this juncture of primordial constitution. Before the terminology of transcendental and empirical, ego and subject, becomes intelligible, the contours of a special world of philosophical discourse need to be sketched. Hence, constitution, as we understand it, is neither the constructionist design of a transcendental ego nor the idiosyncratic conceptualization of an isolated, empirical, thinking self. It is the work of various communities of investigators (scientists, philosophers, artists, and theologians) seeking agreement on common topics of concern.

The above originative understanding of constitution carries with it a more primordial meaning of world than that which has become normative in the tradition of Western epistomology and metaphysics. A long-standing prejudice in Western thought is the metaphysical conceptualization of the world as a collection of entities or properties and relations and the epistemological conceptualization of the world as a totality of propositional facts. This prejudice reaches far back into the tradition, but it received an unprecedented sanction through the institutionalization of the Cartesian concept of *res extensa*. The meaning of world that is at stake in our understanding of the constitution of world by philosophy and the human sciences has more the character of a field or horizon of human concerns. We commonly speak of the "world of the child," the "world of sports," the "business world," and the "academic world." It is this sense of world that is at issue in our question of origin. And it is in this sense of world that we can meaningfully speak of the worlds explored by sociology, psychology, political science, anthropology, linguistics, economics, and history.

These worlds and subworlds can be constituted in such a manner that they mark out rather broad historical and geographical parameters; or they can mark out regions of concern that are somewhat more narrowly specified. For example, the historian may select for his investigative task an exploration of the cultural complex that defines the Byzantine world, or the world of ancient Greece, or the world of the Reformation. His interpretive scheme is constructed so as to thematize specified historical periods and geographical regions. The sociologist may take as his topic of investigation a more geographically restricted horizon of human behavior—for example, the world of the coal miner, the world of the gang, or the world of the family unit. This thematization of world-profiles, and subworlds within these profiles, affords the parameters of the data which are subject to classification, analysis, explanation, and corroboration—which must remain the immediate goal of any special human science.

Within such projects of world constitution, however, we need, as Schutz reminds us, constant recourse to pregiven knowledge and meaning-formation within the originative field of world experience. This recourse is required to keep the special human sciences cognizant of their origin and provide a sheet anchor against the recurring idolatric tendencies on the part of any particular science of man to proffer its world, and the requisite methodology for its explanation, as absolute or paradigmatic. This requirement of a recourse to origin has applicability not only to the human sciences but to the natural sciences as well. Husserl in his celeb-

rated critique of the mathematization of nature had already called
our attention to the occlusion of the life-world which follows in
the wake of the normativization and universalization of the
methodological procedures and practices of the natural sciences.

Joseph J. Kockelmans, proceeding from the cultural critique of
Husserl, has addressed the question of origin more generally, as
pertaining both to the natural and human sciences, in an effort to
provide a general "philosophy of science" that will remain vigilant
of its genealogy. "Each science," Kockelmans writes, "projects its
scientific 'world' in its own way. All the 'worlds' constituted in this
way are different, and one is not more true than the other, at least
in principle. But there is a bond that unites them—the bond
among these 'worlds' consists in their all having been born from
the world immediately lived by the community of men."[9] Each science, be it a natural science or a social science, constitutes its own
world with a prescribed manner of viewing the relevant data and
confirming its hypotheses. Each science affords a perspectival
knowledge of the world, natural or social. And as Kockelmans
points out, there can be no question about the degrees of truth
which might attach to these perspectives. Indeed, in speaking of
the varied worlds constituted by the sciences, the very use of the
concept of truth as a predefined epistemological criterion does not
appear to be particularly profitable. Again, the question of origin
becomes decisive at this point. Out of what shared experience and
pregiven knowledge of nature and society do these constituted
worlds arise? This is the persisting inquiry of radical anthropological reflection.

The understanding of the project of science as a constitution of
a special, thematic world that opens up a perspective on the originary milieu of experience in which a prephilosophical and
prescientific comprehension is already at work will hopefully provide a fresh approach to the traditional and well-augered "problem" of the natural vs. the human sciences. This much discussed
problem, rehearsed by the proverbial "every schoolboy," is for the
most part posed as a methodological issue. Is there one scientific
method, applicable both to the study of nature and the study of
man and society, or do we need separate franchises for the
Naturwissenschaften and the *Geisteswissenschaften*? Now without im-
pugning the legitimacy of methodological analysis and construction, we wish nonetheless to suggest that in the first round of inquiry the matter at hand is one of constitution rather than
methodological design.

The natural sciences as much as the social sciences have their
origin in prescientific concerns and interests. The prescientifically

given knowledge of the life-world continues to inform them both, and they both afford constituted thematic horizons of this life-world. The initial question is thus one of constitution rather than one of methodological correctness or logical validity. The community of investigators in both the natural sciences and the social sciences constitute perspectives on the life-world; however, they constitute their perspectives in a different way. The natural sciences constitute a thematic horizon in which the data under investigation (natural objects and events) do not endow their behavior with meaning. Indeed, it is questionable whether one can speak of the "behavior" of natural objects and events, e.g., the behavior of molecules, without equivocation. In any case, whatever we designate by speaking of the behavior of molecules, we do not purport that they exhibit a behavior which they themselves endow with meaning.

The psychologist, sociologist, anthropologist, and political scientist, on the other hand, constitute a perspective on the life-world in such a manner that the investigatable data are human agents who endow their own gestures, speech, and actions with signification. What is at issue for the human scientist is human actions, motives, purposes, and concerns, which directly and indirectly inform the self-understanding of the agents and actors under investigation. The constituted world of the human scientist is a human world and thus displays a thematic horizon different from that of the natural scientist. Admittedly, it is at this stage that methodological considerations come to the fore; however, the governing directive of these considerations cannot be an abstracted *mathesis universalis* but must rather be that of an epistemic self-reflexivity within the different constituting processes. What the technical logical and methodological design of the particular science will be needs to be determined, but it cannot be determined in an a priori fashion. Only the community of investigators of a particular science can determine it as they work out their data within its constituted thematic horizon. And it is only after this is determined that the question whether indeed there is one logic, two logics, or multiple logics for the varied sciences can first be asked and pursued.

We have spoken at various times throughout the preceding discussion of the demand for a reflexivity on the part of the human sciences. But we have also been critical of the employment of the idealist principle of self-reflexivity in the development of classical philosophical anthropology. Thus it becomes mandatory, if we are to avoid equivocation, to distinguish the principle of self-reflexivity as it is given expression in the idealist tradition from the reflexivity which is at issue in radical anthropological reflection. The principle of self-reflexivity which determines the path of philosophical anthropology from Kant to Husserl follows from a theoretical commitment to a subject of consciousness, defined if you will by playing the transcendental off against the empirical and the empirical off against the transcendental.

The self-reflexivity at issue in this tradition of classical German Idealism, which Husserl sought to surmount but never fully accomplished, was the self-reflexivity of a subject of consciousness yearning for the knowledge of a self that is present to itself. This imputation of power or drive towards self-reduplication provided the idealist model with its epistemological ground. Knowledge of self is the result of a self-reduplication made possible by the self-reflexivity of consciousness. Admittedly, Kant's critical contribution in his *Critique of Pure Reason* was to demonstrate that the project of achieving metaphysical knowledge of the self is saddled with insurmountable epistemic limitations; nonetheless, Kant left the project itself intact. It was simply that the subject's epistemological resources, because of its ineradicable finitude, could not deliver such knowledge, and hence one had to settle for a regulative idea of the self in the absence of constitutive knowledge derived through an application of the categories.

In Hegel's idealism these Kantian epistemic limitations are removed and consciousness as spirit achieves that self-reduplication whereby subject and object are fused into one. The self-consciousness of the cognitive act mediates *that* one knows with *what* one knows so as to produce a coincidence of opposites within the very structure of consciousness. Consciousness as a coincidence of subject and object thus achieves "the self-contained existence of Spirit" and acquires self-mastery. To be sure, in Husserl's transcendental phenomenological idealism, the Hegelian form of synthesis is rejected as is the self-contained character of consciousness. For Husserl it is intentionality rather than a self-contained reflexivity that defines the fundamental character of consciousness. Yet, the telltale marks of idealism remain in Husserl's ascription of a power to consciousness wherewith it is able reflexively to return to its source in the transcendental ego. Consciousness thus has its foundation within itself, and the peculiar task of transcendental phenomenology becomes that of explicating the structure of intentional consciousness vis-à-vis its source, its operative act, and its intended objects.

The subject of self-reflexive consciousness in the above varieties of idealism is defined through the employment of a conceptual scheme that divides the empirical from the transempirical. Self-reflexivity and self-reduplication are powers not of an empirical consciousness but rather of a transcendental self (the Kantian tradition) or a transempirical dialectical mind (the Hegelian tradition). The positioning of consciousness is regulated by the segregation of empirical and nonempirical domains. The empirical is the proper domain for psychological description. Only in the domain of the transcendental or the dialectic of spirit can we discern the fibres and workings of that reflection which is the foundation not only of all knowledge of the self but ultimately also of the world. The analysis of this reflection is the business of philosophy. Hence, we see that with the installation of the transcendental-empirical scaffolding there rides an implicit bifurcation of a science of man on the one hand, entrusted with the task of empirical analysis, and a philosophy of man on the other, proceeding from the standpoint of transcendental analysis. This bifurcation, we suggest, has played a consequential role in the advent of crisis within current scientific and philosophical inquiries into the behavior and being of man.

It might be argued, with considerable support, that Husserl himself, particularly in his later period, recognized the limitations of the idealist theory of consciousness which traveled with the development of transcendental philosophy and that he responded to these limitations by introducing the notion of a pretheoretical functioning intentionality (*fungierende Intentionalität*). Clearly, with this move Husserl opened up an avenue for a critical reassessment of the idealist notion of reflection and the established bifurcation of the transcendental and the empirical. Nonetheless, Husserl was never able to maximize the results of his own discovery and remained committed to the transcendental inquiry standpoint until the very end.

The task of radicalizing fell to his phenomenological successors, and principally the French phenomenologist Maurice Merleau-Ponty. On the basis of his studies of Husserl's later manuscripts, Merleau-Ponty was able to reformulate the direction of phenomenology in such a manner that reflection was liberated from its idealist anchorage in a transcendental mind. Merleau-Ponty's essay "The Philosopher and Sociology" makes the requirement for a radicalization of the phenomenological standpoint explicit: "Reflection is no longer the return to a preempirical subject which holds the keys to the world; it no longer circumambulates its present object and possesses its constitutive parts. Reflection must become aware of its object in a contact or frequenting which at the outset exceeds the power of comprehension. . . . Reflection is no longer the passage to a different order which reabsorbs the order of present things; it is first and foremost a more acute awareness of the way in which we are rooted in them."[10] The borders between the transcendental and the empirical become less and less distinct in this understanding of reflection. Reflection is no longer separable from the order of things into which man is inserted and in which he moves about as perceiver, speaker, and actor. Reflection is wrested from the order of transcendental self-reflexivity and its eternal return to the conditions of knowledge, and liberated from a self-contained closure. Reflection adheres to the world as experienced.

A singularly important feature of Merleau-Ponty's radicalization of the phenomenological standpoint is that reflection bears the explicit inscription of history. The order of things in which reflection is operative is an historical order of things which intrudes into our private and social lives and provides the horizon against which meanings are constituted. Still making use of the transcendental-empirical doublet, in an effort to think beyond it, Merleau-Ponty speaks of the descent of the transcendental into history. "Thus the transcendental descends into history. Or as we might put it, the historical is no longer an external relation between two or more absolutely autonomous subjects but has an interior and is an inherent aspect of their very definition."[11]

In these seminal suggestions, Merleau-Ponty opens a path toward a possible radicalization of the classical, idealist notion of reflection as grounded in the self-reflexive consciousness of a preempirical subject. Particularly what interests us in Merleau-Ponty's suggestions is the anticipated movement beyond the transcendental-empirical doublet toward a more originative reflection, which is already visible in the practical and communicative projects of everyday life. This reflection requires neither the categorial frame of transcendental analysis nor the objective schema of empirical explanations. There is no requirement to return to the epistemological space of a self-reflexive consciousness. The reflection at issue here is the reflection at work in the meaning-establishment and meaning-interpretation of originary world-experience. It is a reflection that rates a site of origin of every science and philosophy of man.

This newly discovered terrain in which originative reflection is at work gives the requirement for reflexivity on the part of the human sciences a new expression. Contrasted with the self-reflexivity demand of classical philosophical anthropology, whereby a philosophical foundation is sought in a structure of self-reflexive consciousness that is able to go out from itself, return to itself, and know itself as subject and object, the reflexivity of radical anthropological reflection marks out a return not to an epistemological ego but to a precategorial world of prephilosophical and prescientific comprehension. A reflexivity upon the world as experienced replaces the interiorized self-reflexivity of a transcendental, epistemological subject attempting to establish the foundations of all knowledge. This demand for a reflexivity on the part of the human sciences, admittedly, reminds us of Whitehead's repeated injunction to avoid the "fallacy of misplaced concreteness." According to Whitehead this fallacy results when an abstraction, methodological or metaphysical, becomes reified and is considered only in terms of its exemplification of categorial thought.[12] Although Whitehead was concerned principally to illustrate the ill effects of this fallacy in its neglect of the sentient qualities in the life of an actual entity, the application of the fallacy could easily be extended to cover the occlusion of the lifeworld which results when a science of man gravitates into the abstract constructionism of pure theory on the one hand, or the abstracted empiricism of reified facts on the other hand.

The radicalization of knowledge that requires this perpetual return to the origin pertains as much to philosophy as a discipline as it pertains to the several human sciences. The project of philosophy itself must come under scrutiny along with the projects and designs of the special sciences. There is a sense in which radical anthropological reflection carries philosophy to its "end," not in the sense of displacing or superseding it by another body of knowledge, but in the sense of thinking it through to its origin. We understand Merleau-Ponty to be moving in this direction when he writes: "Philosophy is not a particular body of knowledge; it is the vigilance which does not let us forget the source of all knowledge."[13] We would prefer, however, to speak of radical anthropology as protophilosophy, given its project of bringing to view the relevance of prephilosophical comprehension in the praxis and poetics of everyday life and language. It is within such a context that our continuing skepticism concerning a search for philosophical foundations needs to be understood. The language of origin replaces the language of philosophical foundations. Epistemological and metaphysical construction, necessary though they may be as natural appetitions of the human mind, are sufficient neither to account for the origin of philosophy nor the origin of the sciences of man.

NOTES

1. "Plessner's Philosophical Anthropology: Implications for Role Theory and Politics," *Inquiry,* Vol. 17, pp. 49–50.

2. See particularly Gehlen, *Der Mensch: Seine Natur und Seine Stellung in der Welt* (Frankfurt-Main: Athenäum Verlag, 1940) and Plessner, *Laughing and Crying: A Study of the Limits of Human Behavior,* trans. Marjorie Grene (Evanston: Northwestern University Press, 1970).

3. For critical discussions touching these and related issues the reader is referred to Christian K. Lenhardt, "The Rise and Fall of Transcendental Anthropology," and Fred R. Dallmayr, "Critical Theory Criticized: Habermas's *Knowledge and Human Interest* and its Aftermath." Both of these articles appeared in *The Philosophy of the Social Sciences,* Vol. 2, No. 3, 1972.

4. See particularly Chapter Nine, "Man and his Doubles," in *The Order of Things* (New York: Random House 1970).

5. Linguistic science, according to Heidegger, can deal only with language in its objective mode and function. The linguistic function of language is understood as the imparting of information. Metalinguistics serves only to provide a metaphysics for this objectifying approach to language. "Metalinguistics is the metaphysics of the permeating technification of all language into the sole functioning interplanetary instrument of information," *Unterwegs zur Sprach,* 3rd edition (Günther Neske Pfullingen, 1965), p. 267.

6. See his essay, "A World of Pure Experience," in *Essays in Radical Empiricism* (New York: Longmans, Green and Co., 1940). The reader is also referred to Calvin O. Schrag, *Experience and Being* (Evanston: Northwestern University Press, 1969), pp. 41–48.

7. *The Phenomenology of the Social World,* trans. George Walsh and Frederick Lehnert (Evanston: Northwestern University Press, 1967), p. 241.

8. *Phenomenology of the Social World,* p. 248.

9. *Phenomenology: The Philosophy of Edmund Husserl and Its Interpretation* (New York: Anchor Books, 1967), p. 550.

10. *Signs,* trans. Richard C. McCleary (Evanston: Northwestern University Press, 1964), pp. 104, 105.

11. *Signs,* p. 107; cf. p. 109: "Since we are all hemmed in by history, it is up to us to understand that whatever truth we may have is to be gotten not in spite of but through our historical inherence. Superficially considered, our inherence destroys all truth; considered radically, it founds a new idea of truth."

12. *Process and Reality* (New York: The Humanities Press, 1929), p. 11.

13. *Signs,* p. 110.

CHAPTER 4

The World of Fact and Value

The ideal of pure theory and the demand for philosophical foundations have directed inquiries not only in the search for the nature of knowledge but also in the recurring attempts to found a secure basis for valuation. Throughout the development of philosophical anthropology, these two concerns have remained in the foreground. A philosophical anthropology of knowledge has always been accompanied by a philosophical anthropology of value, either tacitly or explicitly. As the several human sciences became more specialized and more insular, repeated appeals to value theory were made in the hope of reintegrating the human sciences around a common locus of value. Thus it is not surprising to find the rather common view that the current crisis in the sciences of man is the result of the inability of the human sciences to enter into a proper alliance with the root values of civilization. We need only to recall the vigorous methodological disputations on the topic of a value-free science, so common in the late nineteenth and twentieth century, to recognize how important the question about value has been not only for the philosophy of the human sciences but also for the philosophy of the natural sciences.

More recently, of course, it is fashionable to debate the virtues and vices of technology as it is seen to pose a threat to human values and the quality of human life in general. There are those who find in technology and in technology-oriented science if not the workings of Satan himself at least the well-executed tasks of some of his emissaries. So again we see the recurring tendency to appeal to some species of value theory as a way of dealing with the current predicament. One of the main critical issues that we will raise in this chapter is whether value theory is adequate for the task or whether indeed it is still part of the crisis. The presuppositions and the language of value theory, which define the problem as that of adjusting the relation of fact and value, need to be subject to a radical critique. If we are to see our way clear through the conceptual crises confronting philosophical and scientific studies of man, we will need to complement our radical critique of *theory of knowledge* with a radical critique of *theory of value*.

The path that radical anthropological reflection traverses in its dealing with the problem of value points to the same region that was explored in the preceding chapter, in which the radicalization of knowledge was at issue. This process of radicalization, as we saw, led us to a prephilosophical and prescientific comprehension of the world operating in the speech, motivations, projects, and aspirations of man as he makes his way about in the actual context of human life. We spoke of this context as the world of originary experience, from which the concept construction in scientific explanation and philosophical analysis proceeds. This context of origin, as the habitation of praxis-oriented insight, has a noetic feature. Knowledge is already present in this world of originary experience, although it is neither the categorial knowledge of philosophical analysis nor the knowledge of explanation and prediction supplied by science. We furrowed the path to this world of prephilosophical and prescientific comprehension by way of a deconstruction of the transcendental-empirical framework of inquiry, which has determined the development of philosophical anthropology from its beginnings. This led to a radical critique of the metaphor of philosophical foundations and a replacement of the quest for a unification and integration of the methods and results of the special human sciences with a quest for the origin of scientific and philosophical knowledge of man.

The path pursued by radical anthropology in its handling of the problem of value is similar. Here too we are in quest of a recovery of the origin. This requires a radicalization of value to complement our radicalization of knowledge. What such a radicalization of value is designed to accomplish is a dismanteling of the conceptual scaffolding of traditional value theory through a displacement of the fact-value dichtomy, as our radicalization of knowledge resulted in a thinking beyond the transcendental-empirical dichotomy. As we shall see, at critical points these two dichotomies have fraternized to produce common philosophical mischief. In the history of the discussions of knowledge and value, the dichotomies of fact and value and the empirical and the transcendental have often traveled side by side, even though the travel companions have not always been aware of each other's presence. That there is a connection between these two dichotomies, particularly on the one side of the ledger, ought come as no surprise. Surely the way we construe the meaning of "empirical" will have a profound effect upon our understanding of the meaning of "fact." Empirical knowledge, as it has been understood in the history of empiricism, allegedly provides us with a knowledge of facts. Matters of fact are known through empirical observation and explanation; ideas of relations are apprehended through logical or conceptual analysis. This is the doctrine of traditional empiricism, articulated most eloquently by Hume. And it is this view of empiricism and the corresponding view of fact that have not only informed the post-Humean garden varieties of empiricism, but they have also remained uncontested throughout the influential development of transcendental philosophy.

It should be pointed out that in Kant's celebrated critique of Hume it was not so much Hume's understanding of the perception of empirical fact that was at issue, but rather Hume's neglect of the categorial structure of the human mind wherewith observable facts first became genuinely knowable as proper objects of knowledge. Sense perception, according to Kant, provides us only with a manifold of discrete, Humean sensory appearances. What is required beyond this, argues Kant, is a transcendental synthesis which places the discrete sensory appearances within an organizing category. Transcendental philosophy thus functions more as a *completion* or fulfillment of empiricism than as a critique of its presuppositions concerning the meaning of the empirical and the meaning of fact. Such a critique is precisely what is required in our radicalization of knowledge and value. Kant's critical philosophy on this issue simply was not critical enough. It needs to be radicalized in such a way that it places under critical scrutiny at the same time the meaning of the empirical and the need for the transcendental.

In the preceding chapter, we performed such a process of radicalization by carrying through a critique of transcendental reflection so as to uncover a more originary operation of reflection in the concrete, precategorial life-world. In this chapter, we will continue the process of radicalization by attending to the delivered meanings of "empirical" and "fact" in the hope of tracing their genealogy to a more originative world of experience. Thus we will at the same time complete the deconstruction of the transcendental-empirical doublet and transfigure the empirical meaning of fact in the fact-value doublet so as to make possible an overcoming of this dichotomy also. But as we are forced to do a critical examination of *both* polarizing elements in the transcendental-empirical doublet, so also we must subject to radical scrutiny *both* polarizing elements in the institutionalized fact-value doublet. Hence, our archaeology of the meaning of fact needs be accompanied with an archaeology of the meaning of value. The meaning of value, from the perspective of radical anthropology, is no less problematic than is the meaning of fact. Indeed, in the end the philosophical definition of value trades on its distinction from fact; and the philosophical definition of fact trades on its distinction from value.

A precedent for the proposed radicalization of value, it might be urged, has already been provided by Nietzsche in his renowned "transvaluation of all values" (*Umwertung alle Werte*). Admittedly, Nietzsche was able to complete only the first part of what was intended as his crowning philosophical achievement which was to bear the above title. Nonetheless, a careful reading of Nietzsche's works will show that many of his earlier writings (particularly his *Genealogy of Morals*) were already aimed in this direction. Furthermore, it is difficult to unpack the often veiled meanings of Nietzsche's major motifs (such as the will-to-power, the overman, the eternal recurrence, the death of God, and the role of the Dionysian) without reference to his concern with the problem of value. This is not to say that the transvaluation of value constitutes the dominant and overarching thematic in Nietzsche's philosophy; it is only to say that it is a thematic that he held to be of considerable importance.

The problem of value becomes a "problem" for Nietzsche because of the frightening encroachment of nihilism. "What I relate is the history of the next two centuries. I describe what is coming, what can no longer come differently: *the advent of nihilism.* . . . For why has the advent of nihilism become *necessary*? Because the values we have had hitherto thus draw their final consequence; because nihilism represents the ultimate logical conclusion of our great values and ideals."[1] Nihilism, according to Nietzsche, is imminent. And somewhat ironically, to be sure, the imminence of this nihilism is the logical result of our cherished and revered values! Our values, the values of modern Western man, are now making their appearance in the guise of disvalues. They dull our senses, stifle our creativity, and threaten the fabric of our personal and social existence with a total loss of meaning. This must surely, avers Nietzsche, oblige us to question how this nihilism has come upon us.

Nietzsche himself answers this question by locating the source of nihilism in a platonized Christianity that has constructed an other-worldly moral ideal, buttressed by a metaphysics of theism. Nihilism is the inevitable result of the awareness that such a religio-metaphysical grounding of value is spurious, poetically articulated by Zarathustra's dramatic proclamation of the death of

God. The god of traditional theism is dead, and the values heretofore anchored in a transmundane realm thus become groundless and can now be psychologically explained as the simple consequence of a herd morality regulated by the constraints of the good and bad conscience. This herd morality, with its stultifying table of virtues and commandments of world and life negation, has so permeated Western culture that a disclosure of its true genealogy produces a veritable mood of nihilism. No longer can values be viewed as resting securely on a metaphysically defined religio-moral foundation; they must now be seen as valueless ingredients within the fabric of a life-denying herd morality. Hence, Nietzsche is forced to conclude: "It is in one particular interpretation, the Christian moral one, that nihilism is rooted."[2]

It is against the backdrop of the above definition and diagnosis of nihilism that Nietzsche's proposed transvaluation of value needs to be understood. Properly regarded, the transvaluation of value is Nietzsche's corrective to the conformism and leveling tendencies of a conventionalized Platonic-Christian morality; and it is only through the exercise of such a corrective, Nietzsche believes, that the tide of nihilism can be stemmed. This exercise follows the route toward a new terrain of value-creation. A master morality of the self-affirmative individual replaces the subordinate, slave morality of the herd. This master morality is embodied in Nietzsche's highly symbolical, and unfortunately much maligned, notion of the overman. It is the overman who is able to channel the will-to-power in the direction of a radical self-affirmation, annihilate all hitherto existing values, and create new values which exemplify the courage for self-mastery. This spiritaul struggle requires a transmoral conscience whereby the categories of good and evil, which are simply the speech of the good and bad conscience of the herd, are transcended. Thus the self-affirmation and self-mastery of the overman is achieved "beyond good and evil" through a creative vision that transfigures and transforms the conventional virtues of the Christian moral ideal.

Our current project need not involve us in a detailed analysis and assessment of the particulars in Nietzsche's diagnosis of the problem of nihilism and his recommendation for a cure. Clearly, some troublesome features are present in Nietzsche's proposed program of transvaluation. Of principal interest to us is that Nietzsche saw, more clearly than any other philosopher of his age, that the problem of value is a problem that resides in the genealogy of value itself. What is the origin of value as value? The very language of value-theory may itself be problematic. We simply cannot begin with the assumption that the plethora of conventional codes and norms (social, legal, moral, and religious) already provide us with an unimpeachable mandate for valuation, to which all developments in technology and socio-political formation are answerable. Unfortunately, too often "humanistic" arguments for the humanizing of technology and society are made precisely on such a premise. The crisis of the human sciences, as we have argued, goes deeper than the much discussed *misuse* of technology—although it does assuredly involve that. The crisis is as much a crisis within value theory itself as it is a crisis within the domain of technology. To Nietzsche, who saw this even before the frantic flurry of modern technological development, we owe an inestimable debt.

Although Nietzsche saw clearly enough that value was a problem unto itself, certain impediments, some internal and some external to his thought, precluded a consistent and adequate resolution of the issue. We find two such impediments blocking his path to a radical critique of value. The one has to do with a proclivity toward aestheticism, particularly in his earlier writings, which tended significantly to restrict the parameters of his transvaluation of value. The other has to do with his uncritical acceptance of an empiricist-positivist view of science and fact.

Nietzsche's position as regards aestheticism was admittedly ambiguous. In his first book, *The Birth of Tragedy*, an aestheticist standpoint seems to be fairly clearly stated, epitomized in his well-known epigram: "It is only as an *aesthetic phenomenon* that existence and the world are eternally *justified.*"[3] This early move in the direction of aestheticism may have been occasioned in part by his polemics against Plato and Kant, in which he spiritedly contested Plato's elevation of the Good as the supreme metaphysical principle and Kant's doctrine of the primacy of moral values. An appeal to art and the aesthetical consciousness as a higher mode of existence may at this time in Nietzsche's development have constituted the opportune standpoint from which to counter Plato's subordination of art to the vision of the Good and Kant's centrality of the moral ideal. As his philosophy of the will-to-power matured, however, there is evidence that he became increasingly dissatisfied with his earlier aestheticism. In its existential expression as the power to create, the doctrine of the will-to-power opens the way to an ontology of creativity which transvalues not only traditional moral values but traditional aesthetical values as well. The portrait of the overman in *Thus Spake Zarathustra* is a display of courage and creativity as concrete existential exemplifications of a universal will-to-power. Yet, even in this "classical period" of his philosophy of the will-to-power and the overman, Nietzsche was not wholly successful in resisting the lure of aestheticism. Not only are there in *Thus Spake Zarathustra* recurring examples of artistic creation as illustrations of existential creativity, but also when Nietzsche looks for flesh and blood representatives of the overman ideal it is creative artists rather than thinkers or men of action who are referenced. Therefore, we must conclude that Nietzsche never fully succeeded in surmounting his earlier aestheticism.

The second impediment in Nietzsche's thought that blocked the path to a radical critique of the problem of value was his stance on the nature of fact and the task of science. Nietzsche appropriated, rather uncritically, an empiricistic view of fact and a positivistic concept of science. His reverberating fusillade against metaphysical truth was, on the one hand, launched from the trenches of scientific truth. Science, according to Nietzsche, has the franchise to explain nature; and its method is guided by the objectivity of empirical fact rather than by metaphysical construction. To be sure, Nietzsche was suspicious of scientific attempts at explaining human motivation and action. By his own admission, he learned more about the behavior of man from Dostoevsky than from empirical psychology. Human existence, unlike a fact of nature, is not objectively decipherable. Hence, there is no science of human existence. But it is precisely in this stance that we discern a peculiar confrontation of human existential value with objective scientific fact. For Nietzsche's resolution of this conflict, if we can indeed speak of resolution here, we must turn to his notions of the will-to-power and the overman. The existential expression of the will-to-power in the figure of the overman makes possible not only a mastery of self but also a mastery of nature. Thus Nietzsche, admittedly in a somewhat oblique manner, contributed to the development of the technological picture of nature and the demand for controlling knowledge which is so much a part of the contemporary scientific world view. This occurred, we suggest, because he did not fully grasp the requirement for a radical inquiry into the meaning of fact on the level of prescientific comprehension. The origin of fact, and hence the originative disclosure of nature, remains occluded in Nietzsche's philosophy of the will-to-power.[4]

Marx, like Nietzsche, registered a basic dissatisfaction with traditional philosophical approaches to the problem of value and was able to discern that the main "problem" had to do with the philosophical formulation of the problem itself. And it may well be that Marx with his early notion of praxis as sensuous human activity possessed the requisite resources to surmount the value-theory framework of inquiry with its stifling fact-value dichotomy. But unfortunately this was not to be, mainly because of the development of a Marxist orthodoxy that attempted to incorporate Marxian praxis into a pragmatics of technical control, which regulated both its view of fact and its view of value. Consequently, Marxist orthodoxy moved farther and farther away from a possible access to the origin of fact and value within the lived relations of praxis. Facts, in the guise of production and exchange relations, were pictured as serial objectivities amenable to controlled scientific investigative procedures; and values, understood as economic satisfactions, became technized as instruments for achieving socially desirable goals. Now the Marxists were principally concerned with ferreting out the spurious values of false consciousness, the bourgeoisie values of state and church that functioned as repressive norms. But in their appropriation of Marx's notion of praxis as a principle of redress, the Marxists simply appealed to instrumental values of another stripe, wherewith the repressive norms of bourgeoisie culture would be countered. In such a scheme of things, not only does the source of the values of authentic consciousness remain a problem, but also the issue of the originative disclosure of a world in which valuation first appears as an expression of human concern is submerged.

Given this concomitant technization of value and fact in orthodox Marxism, it is not surprising that the contemporary preoccupation with matters of value and fact should take the form of a *methodological* dispute as to the possibility or impossibility of a value-free science. The volatile *Methodenstreits* of the 1960s, in which Marxists clashed with positivists, did not emerge on the scene as an unexpected phenomenon.[5] The framework in which both positivism and Marxism viewed facts and values was such that a methodological posturing of the issue was inevitable. If facts and values are defined within an objectivist perspective of controlling knowledge, then the "problem of value" becomes that of determining the function of facts and values within a logic of scientific methodology. The guiding question then becomes an inquiry into whether the methodological procedures of science (and in this case specifically the sciences of man) are themselves value-free or value-laden.

Now the requirement posited by radical reflection is not that of further refining the arguments on the one side or the other, but rather that of interrogating the unspoken framework of inquiry which led to the congealing of the issue of fact and value as a methodological problem in the first place. Through this interrogation, a precategorial and premethodological experience of fact

and value can then be uncovered. In the definition of the problem
of value as a methodological concern for the human sciences, tacit
presuppositions of fact and value as objective properties and relations are already put into play. Consequently, the question of the
connection of these abstracted properties and relations becomes
the dominant preoccupation. Can we devise a methodology for
the investigation of fact which remains immune to value claims, or
are value properties and relations already insinuated in the definition and use of facts? As is well known, a plethora of claims and
counterclaims has been offered by the contestants in the academic
fray occasioned by this problem; and some of the onlookers are
profoundly puzzled that no definitive answer to this problem has
as yet been forthcoming. A more genuine puzzlement, we suggest,
is that the problematic character of the problem itself has thus far
evaded scrutiny. Why is the problem of fact vs. value a problem?
And why have we been saddled with the sundry conceptual
conflicts in attempting to deal with this problem? Why has this
particular crisis of methodology been thrust upon us?

This methodological crisis, we suggest, is generated in the very
definition of the problem which trades on a conflation of concepts
drawn from an abstracted empiricism on the one hand and a
technization of value theory on the other. The true character of
this crisis only becomes visible when one moves from the level of
methodological analysis to archaeological inquiry. The crisis is
then seen as the generation of problems resulting from an occlusion of the originary milieu of world experience. What is at issue
ultimately is the question of the *archē* or the origin of fact and
value within the lived relations of man with his social world. It is
this archaeology of fact and value that radical reflection sets as its
major goal in its project of the radicalization of value.

A successful execution of this project rests on the fulfillment of
a double demand for an archaeology of value on the one hand
and an archaeology of fact on the other. Indeed, one cannot proceed without the other, for what happens on the side of our understanding of fact affects our understanding of value, and vice
versa. If our understanding of fact proceeds from an empiricist-
positivist perspective, which has been dominant in modern and
contemporary discussions of the fact-value issue, this understanding will regulate what we do with values. If the meaning of fact is
restricted to the results of controlled observation and verification
as it proceeds in the physical sciences, then clearly value will have
no place within the fabric of fact. Hence, if a place is to be found
for values at all, it will need to be somewhere other than in the
domain of fact—perhaps in the domain of noncognitive, emotive

utterances. This was the form that the argument for an emotivist theory of ethics took during the heyday of positivism. And although it is becoming fashionable today, particularly in philosophical circles, to speak about the death of positivism, we should recognize its rather formidable impact upon nineteenth- and twentieth-century modes of thought.

Positivism tended to shape the inquiry standpoints even of those who rejected it. We observe that on the fact-value issue the antipositivists for the most part tacitly appropriated the positivist understanding of fact and then sought to deal with the problem by making some conceptual adjustments on the value side of the ledger. These adjustments sometimes involved the installation of a special nonempirical mode of apprehension, a "moral consciousness," which was granted the legitimacy to exist alongside the empirical apprehension of matters-of-fact. At other times, the adjustments took the form of recasting the "nature" of values, construing them variously as intuitable essences, undefinable qualities, ends in view, obligatory acts, or linguistic performances. But all of these adjustments, ingenious though they may be in their own right, still proceed within the ruminations of value theory as it works with an abstracted empiricism. Hence, an archaeological reflection on the meaning of fact assumes such considerable importance. Any program of a radicalization and transvaluation of value cannot productively proceed without it. The failure of Nietzsche's projected transvaluation of value, for example, must ultimately be seen in terms of its neglect to carry through simultaneously a transfiguration of the meaning of fact.

The conceptual framework which occasioned the abstracted empiricism of positivism was one in which facts were viewed as discrete, atomistic, and nonintentional. In this conceptual framework, the physico-neurological model of perception became paradigmatic; and perception was understood as the reception of discrete, isolated, and contingent physical properties. Consequently it was necessary for positivism to construct a theory of meaning and a theory of language which would be able to accommodate these facts by ordering them within the propositional forms of a truth-functional logic. This uncritical use of truth-functional logic in the service of an abstracted empiricism further contributed to the picturing of facts as discrete, isolated, contingent, and nonintentional. But facts so defined are already abstractions from the flow of lived-through experience as it emerges and develops in a concrete life-world. William James, in his trenchant attack on traditional empiricism, already discerned the abstractive fallacy that was at work in this conceptual

framework and urged a return to "the world of pure experience."[6] Empiricism, according to James, pulverized this originary
world of experience by construing it as a discontinuous succession
of discrete sensations and, consequently, concealed the
intentionality-laden conjunctions present in every undivided por-
tion of experience. Experience, in James's *radical* empiricism, is a
field of consciousness with expanding fringes, rather than a collection of discrete sensorial facts received by an isolated subject
who then orders them through the implementation of a logic of
propositions. As a result we are able to discern in James's seminal
explorations of the world of pure experience a radical questioning
of the abstracted view of fact in traditional empiricism and positivism and a movement in the direction of our previously articulated originary matrix of world-experience.

The view of fact in abstracted empiricism, as we have noted
above, has been uncritically appropriated by some of the staunch-
est opponents of positivism. A particularly noteworthy example is
the existentialist Jean-Paul Sartre. According to Sartre,

> If we ask ourselves what a fact is, we see that it is defined by that
> which one should *meet* in the course of an investigation and that it
> always presents itself as an unexpected enrichment and a novelty in
> relation to anterior facts. It is therefore not necessary to count on the
> facts to organize themselves in a synthetic totality which by itself
> might yield its meaning. . . . To expect the *fact* is, by definition, to
> expect the isolated, to prefer, because of positivism, the accidental to
> the essential, the contingent to the necessary, disorder to order; it is,
> on principle, to cast what is essential into the future.[7]

Here Sartre seems rather willing to concede the positivist's
definition of fact. The implications of this concession for Sartre's
comprehension of the task of the human sciences, and particularly
psychology, are far-reaching. According to Sartre, psychology is
destined to work with facts, positivistically defined as isolated, accidental, and nonintentional: "Psychology, insofar as it claims to
be a science, can furnish only a sum of miscellaneous facts, most
of which have no connection with the others."[8] Empirical psychology is restricted to an investigation of contingent and nonintentional facts. As such it is unable to deal with issues of meaning and
value, which in Sartre's scheme of things fall within the domain of
phenomenological eidetic analysis. Hence, Sartre is forced to install a special discipline of phenomenological psychology which
first is able to broach the problem of meaning and thus ensure the
humanistic character of psychology. As it is set up by Sartre, the
problematic trades on the bifurcation of fact and essence (mean-

ing); and in this respect, he remains true to the method of phenomenological reduction as it was formulated in the earlier writings of Edmund Husserl. In his early statement of the reduction, Husserl too was not yet wholly liberated from a posivitistic view of fact; hence, he needed recourse to his doctrine of the *Wesensschau* which would enable us to isolate through a procedure of eidetic reduction those structures of meaning which provide the essential and necessary conceptual fibres that can never be delivered through an investigation of mere facts. It is precisely this fact-essence bifurcation, with its invitation that we look for values on the side of essences, that needs be subject to a radical critique. The root of the crisis in the current sciences of man, we submit, resides not in a state of affairs in which the special sciences, defined as custodians of empirical fact, are unable to recognize the need for another special discipline which might provide them with the secure philosophical foundation of a doctrine of essence (and no matter that in this case the essences are phenomenologically rather than metaphysically understood). The installation of the fact-essence dichotomy is itself a part of the crisis and requires a dismantling so that a more originative posturing of meaning-establishment and formation can be brought to light. The crisis of the human sciences, we reiterate, is occasioned by the occlusion of this originative posture. This is the loss of reflexivity on the part of the human sciences of which we spoke earlier. In this originative posture, facts have not yet congealed into discrete and atomistic entities and meanings have not yet congealed into essences. If we are here to speak the language of facts at all, then it is to be made clear that it is "world-facts" as part of the fabric of world-experiencing disclosure that is at issue.[9]

World-facts, as distinct from the facts of an abstracted empiricism, are configurative rather than atomistic in character. They are present in world experience as figures with horizontal backgrounds. The world-facts of perception and human action are presented not as discrete data but as experienced totalities in which figure and background are interwoven. Perceptions and human actions comport horizontal backgrounds that enter into the meaning of the object as perceived and the action as enacted. The book is perceived as being on a table which is set against the wall. This residing on a table that is outlined against a wall provides a copresent background or horizon that marks out the setting for the appearance of the book. Likewise the figuration of a human activity, such as an act of political rebellion, takes shape against a background of social institutions and practices which bear directly on the significance of the act itself. So-called perceptual and social facts are thus never isolated occurrences. They require for their very appearance as experienced facts the background of a natural and a social world. The manner in which they appear displays a copresence of figure and background. This is the first feature of the configurative character of world-facts that needs to be articulated.

World-facts, however, are configurative in another respect. As *experienced* world-facts, they implicate an experiencer. The experiencer is part of the configuration. The perceiver is part of the world-fact of perception, and the rebel is part of the world-fact of social rebellion. Both the perceiver and the rebel bring with them a personal history which in some manner shapes the event. The meaning-formation at work in world-facts requires not only the insinuation of the multiple horizons that line the natural and social world, but also the contributions of an experiencer who remains within the fabric of world-fact. It is important to underscore that on this level there can be no talk about a "doctrine of self" that sets the self in opposition to the world, or even a philosophy of consciousness, particularly if this philosophy of consciousness trades on a separation of consciousness from the body. The experiencer is neither disembodied nor is he marked off from the world through the implementation of that problematic disjunction of "objective" vs. "subjective" facts. The experiencer is inseparable from the configurative presence of world-facts. The seminal contributions of William James on this point, and the more systematic and detailed phenomenological analysis of the perceptual world and the lived-body by Merleau-Ponty, already comprise substantive accomplishments in the direction of an understanding of world-fact. Without their explorations, our recovery of the origin of the human sciences and philosophical anthropology would be manifestly more difficult.

A third distinguishing feature of world-facts, as contrasted with the view of fact in abstracted empiricism, is their meaning-bearing character. World-facts are already imbued with sense or significance. They display an intentional structure in which understanding and interpretation are already operating. Proceeding in this vein, Michael Polanyi has given studied attention to the misreading of fact in abstracted empiricism and has concluded that "science is not a mere collection of facts, but a system of facts based on their scientific interpretation."[10] According to Polanyi, operative in the project of science is a *logic of tacit knowing* that precedes the formalized logic of explanation. This logic of tacit knowing characterizes science as a *human activity*. It is an originative and persisting feature of scientific cognition, discernible al-

ready in the most elementary stages of a scientific comprehension
of the fabric of fact and operative throughout the entire process
of the doing of science.[11]

This broadened posturing of the texture of fact allows for a
discernment of the meaning-establishment and meaning-
formation that occurs within the configurative complex of
experiencer-figure-background. The experiencer, as perceiver
and actor, conspires as it were with figure and background to establish meaning. Fact and meaning are thus inseparable in the
sphere of world-fact. In the precategorial (presubjective and
preobjective) genesis of meaning that takes place in this sphere,
the bifurcation of the contingent and the essential has not yet
been installed. The abstraction of facts as contingent and disor-
dered and the reification of meaning as a realm of essences are
the result of a second order movement of conceptualization. On
the abstracted level, facts are split off from meanings; but in the
sphere of world-facts, meaning and fact mix and mingle. Every
world-fact of perception is already a comprehension of the world
in some manner. The world-facts that become manifest in man's
use of tools and utensils appear within a field of practical concerns.[12] The world-facts of socio-political action are facts which
already endow the action with meaning. Here the sphere of action
is at the same time the sphere of sense. Clearly the meaning or
sense at issue is not that of an abstract verification theory of meaning which necessarily follows from an abstract localization of fact,
but rather a precategorial and preobjective deployment of meaning within the synthetic totality of experiencer, figure, and
background.

Another noteworthy feature of world-facts is their attunement
with the articulative and expressive function of ordinary language. This should come as no surprise insofar as the genesis of
meaning in the precategorial life-world, with its multiple horizons
of perceptual profiles and perspectives of action, is *set forth* by language. But this language is itself precategorial and preobjective. It
is the language of everyday discourse in the workday world of
human concerns. John Wild has given attention to this close connection between world-facts and ordinary language in his article
"Is There a World of Ordinary Language?" Ordinary language,
argues Wild, is concerned with facts of a different order than
those of a formalized science. There is a world of ordinary language that displays patterns of meaning that are not yet solidified
into the abstract generalizations of scientific language or the universal categories of philosophical language. Wild works out the
connection between world-facts and linguistic usage from an illuminating example:

Let us now turn to a world fact such as: this yellow pencil is now on the table at my right. The pencil is now here before me as I face the world. . . . General terms, of course, like "pencil," "yellow," and "table" have to be used. Otherwise the fact would remain ineffable. But the fact is individual and concrete, as is indicated by the demonstrative words *this* and *my*. The universal terms are used not to express a universal connection, but to illuminate an individual situation here and now which must constantly be recognized and held in mind, if this fact is to be properly analyzed and understood. Here the movement is not only from the concrete to the abstract and universal, but also from the abstract and universal back again to the concrete, which is always the center of attention. Such an entity, in its full concreteness, like this pencil, or me, myself, is always envisaged in the world horizon, though this is often left unexpressed.[13]

The defining feature of world-fact, according to Wild, lies in its "full concreteness." One might push the analysis further at this stage and flesh out the meaning of concreteness by calling attention to the root meaning of *concrescere*, to grow together, which governs the English derivation. The concrete is that which is in the process of growing together. Whitehead is one of the few contemporary philosophers who was able to grasp and utilize this originative sense of concreteness in his doctrine of the concrescence of actual entities. Within the framework of our elucidation of world-fact, that which "grows together" in the full concreteness of perceptual and social facts is the experiencer, figure, and background. This, as we have seen, comprises the configurative character of world-fact. As Wild points out, the demonstrative word "my" in the ordinary language articulation of the world-fact, "This yellow pencil is now on the table at my right," implicates the experiencer within the fabric of world-fact. The demonstrative "this" indicates the concreteness of the figure (the pencil), outlined against the background of being "on the table at my right." It is also noteworthy that ordinary language concretizes universal terms and thus obviates their reification. The indicated direction here is from the concrete to the universal and from the universal back again to the concrete. Thus the concrete is rendered intelligible and communicable. The development of meaning is already present in the sphere of world-facts.

So, when the social scientist speaks about "scientific facts" pertaining to attitude formation, social roles, feelings of nationalism, or primitive practices, these "scientific facts," properly understood, are abstractions from a primordial concrescence of world-facts. To be sure, the social scientist, qua scientist, is required to thematize various profiles of experienced world-facts and subject them to scientific analysis and explanation. Yet these thematizations, if they are to retain their full explanatory force, should not be severed from the originary matrix of world-facts whence they arise. They need to be reinserted, as it were, into the density of lived-through human thought, language, and action. Again we see illustrated the requirement for a reflexivity on the part of the several sciences of man in their efforts to articulate the varied profiles of man and society.

Our radicalization of the meaning of fact, inspired in part by the radical empiricism of William James, has proceeded along the lines of a critique of abstracted empiricism, which in turn has led us to the sphere of concrete world-facts. In this movement from the objectivized and pulverized facts of abstracted empiricism to the full concreteness of experienced world-fact, a happy encounter occurs—an encounter with a precategorial world-valuation. The meaning-formation that is at work in the configurative presence of world-facts is at the same time a process of value-formation. Within the sphere of world-facts, fact and value are inseparable. The genesis of value has its location in that endowment of meaning by the experiencer in his perceptions and actions which we discerned to be part of the fabric of experienced world-facts. Thus it is on this originative level of precategorial meaning-formation that fact and value are equiprimordial. The recovery of this level, however, requires not only a dismantling of the epistemological and methodological scaffolding of an abstracted empiricism but also a deconstruction of traditional value-theory. The drive to recover the originary matrix of world experience requires a concomitant transfiguration of fact and transvaluation of value. Both the value side and the fact side of the institutionalized fact-value dichotomy need to be subject to radical critique.

In the development of Western philosophy, value theory or axiology came to be defined as one of the areas or branches of philosophy, alongside logic, epistemology, and metaphysics. In the course of time, value theory was itself subdivided, sectioned off into a study of moral values (ethics), aesthetical values (aesthetics), and religious values (history and philosophy of religion). Not only is there an evident arbitrariness in such a taxonomy of the branches and special areas of philosophy, but it also opens the door to certain tacit prejudices regarding their proper ordination. There is a long-standing tradition in academic philosophy that logic, epistemology, and metaphysics constitute the "core" of philosophical studies. These three branches have traditionally been viewed as the custodians of reflection on validity, knowledge, and reality, constituting the tribunal before which the various subdisciplines are justified.

There is also a long-standing tradition within this "core" tribunal that the categorial framework of substance-attribute and the
subject-predicate mode of thought provide the proper stance for
philosophical analysis. The implications of this stance for value
theory have been profound. Within such a framework, values become attributes or properties of things or human acts.
Grammatically, they function as predicates assigned to a
grammatical subject. The unspoken presupposition is that we
must first decide what a thing or a human act is, and then we can
determine what kind of value it might have. Value predicates are
later accidental additions that somehow attach to a predetermined
descriptive fact or state of affairs. Thus they remain extrinsic to
the order of things and actions and enter into relation with things
and human actions only via the instrumentation of human desires,
volitions, and appetitions. Good and evil become properties of
things and human actions. Assigned to human actions, they are
viewed as desires or volitions which a human agent or human
group might or might not possess. They are viewed as adventitious or accidental properties—and no matter at this point whether
they be designated as analyzable or unanalyzable properties.

The attempt to so conceptualize values as properties invites the
troublesome metaphor of possession. A value is "something" that
a human agent *owns, possesses,* or *has.* The implication in the
metaphor of possession is that value is determined by *having* relations rather than *being* relations. Here we discern the genealogy of
the separation of value from fact, as this occurs on the side of
value theory. But this separation of fact and value as an implication of value theory cannot be dissociated from the separation of
fact and value as an implication of abstracted empiricism. Indeed
in the final analysis, the one trades on the other. If the understanding of fact is restricted to the framework of an abstracted
empiricism, then the descriptive factualities concerning things and
human actions will preclude any insinuation of value into the fabric of fact. Correspondingly, if the understanding of value finds
its touchstone in a metaphysics of substance and attribute and a
subject-predicate epistemology, then a bifurcation of fact and
value would also seem to be inevitable.

The bifurcation of fact and value thus rests on a double
mistake—a mistake on the side of the understanding of fact and a
mistake on the side of the understanding of value. Facts are misread as abstract generalized propositions about isolated, discrete,
atomistic, and nonintentional states of affairs and, hence, the
configurative and intentional character of world-fact is concealed.
Values are misread as accidental properties bearing an external
relation to things and human acts, and a corresponding conceal-

ment of the unity of fact and value in world experience takes place. And as in the recovery of the fabric of world-fact, we found that facts are not so readily separable from an intentionality-laden horizon or background and a meaning-endowing experiencer; so in our recovery of world-valuation, we now find that values are not so readily separable from things and human acts. The embodied experiencer as living agent is not separated from his value-laden acts, reified as value-predicates. He does not *have* his acts; he *is* as he acts, or he *exists* in his acts. Relations of being take priority over relations of having. The originary setting or milieu of human thought, language, and action is at the same time a horizon of world-values. Patterns of satisfaction and dissatisfaction, approval and disapproval, the obliging and the nonobliging are inseparable from the being and behavior of man and the life of an historical culture. These patterns of valuation are situated in the *lived*-through experiences of self and society. The vigilance of radical reflection keeps these patterns of valuation from congealing into the abstracted entities of attributes and properties that have informed the history of value theory. It reinserts value into the woof and warp of human action and communication. It teaches us to see valuation as a mode of existing in the world.

The peculiar result of our project of radical reflection on fact and value is that it has opened up a vista for looking beyond the institutionalized fact-value dichotomy—not from above but from below. As already in our radicalization of knowledge, so also in our radicalization of value we are led to an originary matrix of precategorial world experience. This precategorial world experience is the sphere of origin in which configurative, intentional world-fact and world-valuation mix and mingle. It is from this presence of world that the various sciences of man receive their motivation; and if there is to be any talk of success here, it must be said that the success of these sciences is measured by the degree to which their special thematizations contribute to an understanding of this presence of world.

NOTES

1. *The Will to Power*, trans. W. Kaufmann and R. J. Hollingdale (New York: Vintage Books, 1968), pp. 3, 4.

2. *Ibid.*

3. *The Birth of Tragedy*, trans. W. Kaufmann (New York: Vintage Books, 1967), p. 52.

4. Habermas recognizes Nietzsche's inability to extricate himself from a positivist understanding of science, put in the service of a technical control over nature, when he says: "Nietzsche conceives science as the activity through which we turn 'nature' into concepts for the purpose of mastering nature. The compulsion to logical correctness and empirical accuracy exemplifies the constraint of the interest in possible technical control over objectified natural processes and, thereby, the compulsion of preserving existence," *Knowledge and Human Interests,* trans. J. J. Shapiro (Boston: Beacon Press, 1971), p. 296.

5. An informative collection of essays dealing with the central issues in this debate has been compiled by T. W. Adorno under the title, *Der Positivismusstreit in der deutschen Soziologie* (Neuwied: Luchterhand Verlag, 1971).

6. See particularly *Essays in Radical Empiricism,* Ch. 2 (New York: Longmans, Green and Co., 1912).

7. *The Emotions: Outline of a Theory,* trans. B. Frechtman (New York: Philosophical Library, 1948), p. 5.

8. *Ibid.*

9. I am indebted chiefly to John Wild in my use of the notion of "world-fact." Assuredly, William James had already pointed to the terrain which is here under exploration; however, it was John Wild who first delineated with some care the distinction between world-facts and abstracted scientific facts in his article "Is There a World of Ordinary Language?", first published in *The Philosophical Review* (67, 4, 1958) and then reprinted in *Existence and the World of Freedom* (Englewood Cliffs: Prentice-Hall, Ind., 1963).

10. *Knowing and Being,* ed. Marjorie Grene (University of Chicago Press, 1969), p. 65.

11. See particularly *The Tacit Dimension* (New York: Doubleday, 1966) and *Personal Knowledge* (New York: Harper Torchbooks, 1958).

12. On this point the reader is referred to Heidegger's illuminating discussion of the posturing of a prephilosophical comprehension of world through the activities of "practical concern" (*Besorgen*). See particularly *Being and Time,* trans. John Macquarrie and Edward Robinson (New York: Harper & Row, 1962), pp. 95– 107.

13. *Existence and the World of Freedom,* pp. 50, 51.

CHAPTER 5

Understanding and Reason: Towards a Hermeneutic of Everyday Life

Our radicalization of knowledge and value, through which a prephilosophical and prescientific posture of knowing and valuing is restored, now sets a final demand before us This demand is occasioned by the recognition that the process of understanding within the precategorial meaning-formation of an originary experiencing of the world is already a project of inter-pretation. Understanding thus develops as an *interpretive* under-standing, and this makes the topic of hermeneutics unavoidable for radical anthropological reflection. This interpretive under-standing works with an expanded expression of reason, which en-compasses the pretheoretical intentionality and lived-through meanings that appear after the doublet of transcendental reflection and empirical explanation has been deconstructed. On the hither side of this doublet, we find a more vibrant and less abstract deployment of reason than formal philosophy has been wont to recognize. Interpretive understanding collaborates with a dynamic and developing reason that resonates through the mo-tives, perceptions, projects, and embodied speech of human agents. But this is not the reason of pure theory, which in its stance of a godlike survey seeks to unify the order of things from above. It is reason inserted into the destiny of the actual context of human life. Hence, the hermeneutical considerations which guide our assessment of this interpretive understanding and this expanded notion of reason point in the direction of a hermeneu-tic of everyday life. Such a hermeneutic not only provides the point of departure for any future ontology of man, it also articu-lates the horizon out of which the special human sciences develop. The human sciences, as disciplined studies of the life of man and his institutions, draw their data from a background of interpreta-tions which permeate the thought and praxis of everyday life.

A hermeneutic of everyday life, which we see as a culmination of radical reflection, has some distinguishing general features. The literature on hermeneutical theory is already vast and still continues to grow. It is not our task here to review this literature in its historical development from Aristotle's *Peri hermeneias* to Gadamer's *Wahrheit und Methode*.[1] Rather our concern is to delineate a new focus on the hermeneutical problem, opened up by radical reflection.

Our proposed recovery of an originary, precategorial matrix of world experience requires first of all a shift from the hermeneutical theory of textual-philological analysis and interpretation to a wider hermeneutic of man's socio-historical existence. The textual model of hermeneutical theory, institutionalized principally by Schleiermacher and Dilthey, needs to be broadened in such a manner as to incorporate into its scope the spoken word as well as the written word. It needs to be extended to include the sphere of perception and its comprehension of the world as well as the transmission of ideational contents. It demands an inclusion of the reading of nature as well as historically delivered texts. It is as much required for an understanding of the project of science as for an understanding of the various programs in the humanistic disciplines. Such a hermeneutic is unavoidable if one is to achieve clarification of the interests and goals of any science of man.

Although we propose a shift away from the textual model of traditional hermeneutical theory, a metaphorical employment of this model may contribute something towards an elucidation of the general design of a hermeneutic of everyday life. Although we might be straining the metaphorical reach of "text," we would not, I think, be stretching it beyond its elastic limits by using the term as an oblique designator of the *texture* of lived-through world experience. It is this texture of everyday life that becomes the "text" in our extended hermenuetic. This text, in our metaphorical extension of the term, is to be approached at the same time as a *con*-text, in the root signification of *contexere,* a weaving together, and in this case a weaving together of the tissues of concern and interest that run through the experience of the personal and the social alike. Everyday life is a context of connections and conjunctions which surface not only in the intentionality of thought but also in the circumspection of practical engagements within an economic and social order. The chief virtue of the language of context in this connection is that it helps to articulate and hold in mind the configurative character of world-fact, vis-à-vis its experiencer-figure-background structure that we sought to explicate in the preceding chapter. However, already at this juncture of our analysis of the operation of interpretative understanding, we note that the context of everyday life exhibits discontinuities and disjunctions as well as connections and conjunctions; and any hermeneutic of everyday life that is to succeed in its project will need to be attentive to these discontinuities and disjunctions. They too bear a significance for an understanding of man's personal and social history.

This shift of the hermeneutical issue to the text of everyday life relocates the traditional problematic in a rather decisive manner. We are here no longer dealing with a literary text as an accomplished fact, but rather with an ongoing life activity in which human agents endow their perceptions and actions with meaning. The phenomenon at stake in the project of interpretive understanding is itself a process of self-understanding and self-interpretation. We must distinguish two levels of interpretive understanding. There is the primordial level of interpretive understanding which is an ongoing process in the precategorial meaning-formation and meaning-establishment that characterizes the concernful preoccupations of daily affairs. Then there is the second-order level of interpretive understanding as a feature of the methodological design in any philosophical or scientific investigation of man and his social world. The difficult task of any philosophy and any science of man is thus the working out of an interpretation of that which is itself a process of interpreting. The success of any execution of such a task can be measured only by the degree to which such a second order of interpretation remains reflexive upon the primordial level of interpretive meaning-formation. This is again to place before the philosophical and scientific studies of man the requirement for a reflexivity that reestablishes the proper liaison with their origin.

The blurring of the above distinction between interpretive understanding as an experiential feature of everyday existence and interpretive understanding as part of the method of philosophical and scientific investigation has ushered in numerous misrepresentations and caricatures of what is addressed when the question of hermeneutics is asked. Both the critics and proponents of hermeneutical theory have contributed to these distortions. At the heart of these distortions is the recurring tendency to construe interpretive understanding principally as a method in competition with the methods of scientific explanation and prediction. The fate of hermeneutics, given this construal of its character, has been rather dismal. The proponents of hermeneutics as a method have been saddled with the enormously difficult task of sorting out the defining methodological (logical and epistemological) principles of hermeneutics, in terms of their distinctions from if not direct opposition to the methodological principles of scientific explanation. Correspondingly, the friends of scientific explanation have either straight-way banished hermeneutics as a method or have tested their generosity by admitting hermeneutics to the anteroom of scientific observation and explanation. At best, interpretive understanding, in the minds of its critics, has been allowed to function as a heuristic device for the preliminary "guesswork" that goes into the formulation of hypotheses relevant to the causal determinants of human behavior. In short, it has been construed as a sort of "psychological sense" which could help to set the stage for rigorous scientific explanation.

A number of misconceptions and prejudices are discernible in this methodological definition of the hermeneutical task. First is the misconception that interpretive understanding has to do with a psychological rapport between the observer and the observed. It were as though the observer has a peculiar technique for entering into the psyche of the observed, peering into its depths, and dredging out its veridical contents. This misconception, we must hasten to add, has been nurtured not only by the critics but also by the advocates. Its source is found principally in the misconstrual of *empathy* as a psychological feeling which is then elevated to the status of an epistemological principle. The language of empathy and empathic identification is undeniably in the literature of hermeneutical theory, both in that of its phenomenological and nonphenomenological proponents. Dilthey himself made considerable use of it, and it would be fair to say that he was not completely innocent with respect to its psychologistic distortion. Given the strong psychologistic connotations of the term, particularly in English, we would recommend, if not its deletion from hermeneutical inquiry, extreme care in its employment so as not to confuse it with a discrete and contingent psychological event. To be sure, Husserl uses the term extensively in his *Cartesian Meditations* and his *Crisis of the European Sciences and Transcendental Phenomenology.* But in Husserl the nonpsychological signification of the term is secured by virtue of his celebrated attack on psychologism in his *Logical Investigations.*

Another feature of the misconception of hermeneutics as a methodological technique relates to certain uncritical attitudes regarding the nature of scientific explanation and the nature of empirical fact. Dilthey himself, certainly one of the more influential contributors to hermeneutical theory, was not yet wholly liberated from an uncritical attitude toward science as an untroublesome project of explaining nature by appeals to lawlike regularities and causal determinants. "Nature we explain; man we understand," says Dilthey.[2] Here the stage is set for that well-known scenario in which the forces of the *Naturwissenschaften* battle with the forces of the *Geisteswissenschaften* — a scenario for which the final score has not yet been written. At most what has been composed thus far is a kind of "standoff" in which science remains entrenched in its cybernetics and the humanistic studies hold the line with their hermeneutics. Max Weber wrestled with this problem in his remarkable work *Economy and Society,* but he was unable to bring it to a resolution because of his own move toward a bifurcation of observational understanding (*aktuelles Verstehen*) and explanatory understanding (*erklärendes Verstehen*).[3] Explanation for Weber comprised a superior mode of understanding, whereby the interpretive contents of observational understanding are explained through a determination of causal connections and subsumption under statistical laws. Interpretive, observational understanding remains incomplete and insufficient by itself and requires supplementation by a more rigorous explanation of the "subjective meaning" of human motives and actions. Although Weber did not solidify this distinction between observation and explanation into a clear and distinct dichotomy, he did devalue the intrinsic worth of interpretive understanding by subordinating it to the requirement for a species of causal explanation that was still informed by certain presuppositions of positivistic science. Hence, it was not surprising that certain representatives of positivistic and empiricistic social science could find in Weber's general perspective an oblique legitimation of their requirement that all observation facts be subsumed under general causal laws. But precisely what remains problematic in such a scheme of things is the uncritical view of fact, which sets the requirement for the procedures of alleged scientific explanation. What is occurring here is a facile transformation of configurative, intentionality-laden *world*-fact into the discrete observable facts of an abstracted empiricism. As we saw in the previous chapter, it is just this abstracted empiricism which needs to be surmounted so that the originary texture of experienced world-fact can be permitted to show itself in its primordial manner of appearing. We find Schutz's critique of Weber on this issue to be right on target. According to Schutz, Weber was forced to treat human motives and actions as *accomplished facts* rather than as *ongoing* motivation and action.[4] Facts then became congealed as abstract, observable properties and isolated and contingent psychic states, requiring some species of causal explanation for their intelligibility. But the world-facts of human action already exhibit a certain comprehension, a praxis-oriented and prescientific "seeing," through which sense borne by interpretive understanding enters the world.

In this shift of attention to the intentionality-laden world-facts of lived experience, we at the same time surmount the prejudices of abstracted empiricism and relocate hermeneutics as an experiential feature of the cognition and interest that unfolds in man's prephilosophical and prescientific comprehension of the social and cultural world. The misconception of viewing hermeneutics principally as a peculiar method employed by the human sciences for selecting, describing, and interpreting their data is thus overcome. However, the proper placement of hermeneutics as a cognitive deployment of meaning within the actual context of daily human affairs does not immunize it from methodological implications. This placement of hermeneutics pertains only to its primordial or first-level expression.

There is also, as we have indicated, a second level of interpretive understanding that attaches to the very project of doing a science or philosophy of man. On this level hermeneutics takes the form of an interpretation of that which is itself an ongoing process of interpretation, and it is on this level that methodological issues are unavoidable. The actual procedures of investigation and analysis by the several human sciences require appropriate methodological designs. Our demand for reflexivity upon the originary world of pure experience does not displace the necessity for methodological constructs; it only installs a vigilance over the precategorial domain of knowledge and human interests so that we may guard against its occlusion and remain cognizant of the source of all constructionist designs, methodological and metaphysical. As such, reflexivity neither invalidates methodology nor does it legislate a nomothetic methodological rule for all the human sciences. It allows for a plurality of methodologies. There are many ways of seeing the world, and there are many ways of doing science and philosophy. What is required is that the methodological principles that inform the doing of science and philosophy not sever the phenomena from the method. In this connection, we are reminded of Lotze's helpful note of caution in the introduction to his *Metaphysics,* where he advises the reader that the "continual sharpening of the knife becomes tedious when there is nothing to cut."[5] The ongoing self-interpretation within human motivation, thought, and action should solicit the method; the method should not prejudge the phenomena. If the origins are not to be occluded, the phenomena should be permitted to speak for themselves and thus guide the construction of methodological theory and procedure. The consequences of this rejection of the primacy of methodology is that methodology is no longer the absolute presupposition of inquiry but is itself a part of the "experimental" furniture.

The human scientist needs to experiment with various methodologies, testing time and again their serviceability. A pragmatic attitude is required so as to keep the question of utility and technique from congealing into a dogmatic assertation of epistemological first principles. The question "How should the human scientist approach his data?" is a question that needs to be asked time and again because of the ongoing and multidimensional character of the phenomenon of social reality and the finite perspective of the investigator. It is thus that the variety of methodologies in the human sciences that have been proposed in recent times is not in itself a regrettable state of affairs, so long as we understand the variegated spectrum of methodologies to be offering experimental and provisional procedures. But it would be a mistake to institutionalize any one methodological approach as the official entrance gate to knowledge of the social world. The adequacy of each particular methodology needs to be determined in the context of the actual practice of each human science as it seeks to work out an understanding and comprehension of its selected phenomena. And the critique of methodology should remain a continuing task, not as a professionalized game of abstract analysis of principles, but as a rigorous conceptual and linguistic analysis of the actual performances within the republic of any particular human science.

Our relocation of interpretive understanding as an ongoing process within the stream of everyday life, which is older than the constructionism of methodology and metaphysics, forces us to readdress the traditional problem of the role of reason. The ideal of rationality has guided philosophical reflection since the time of the Greeks, and the foundations of first principles which philosophical analysis and speculation have sought to establish are foundations which allegedly were to be secured with the durable mortar of reason. The metaphor of foundations has always been informed, tacitly if not explicitly, by an ideal of rationality. Our reassessment of the metaphor of foundations, as employed by formal philosophy, requires a concomitant reassessment of the character, role, and range of reason. Reason itself, particularly in our time, has become a problem. We can no longer proceed with an untroublesome concept of reason as the ground of philosophical and scientific knowledge. We must submit reason itself to a radical critique.

The pathway to such a radical critique, it will be quickly called to our attention, was already opened up by Kant. This is assuredly true. Yet, the problematic as it was set by Kant, particularly in the *Critique of Pure Reason,* was that of an overextension of a categorial use of reason in any effort to establish veridical foundations for traditional metaphysics. His critique was, if you will, a critique of the metaphysical use of reason. But this critique was still launched from an epistemological standpoint in which a criterion of validity, a theory of judgment, and a doctrine of the categories were called upon to adjudicate matters of knowledge. In this respect Kant remained a child of the Age of the Enlightenment. Kant's notion of understanding (*Verstand*) was still placed in the service of a transparent, objectifying mode of thinking and received an explicit categorial expression. And the range of reason (*Vernunft*) was determined in accordance with the categorial operations of the understanding. In our relocation of understanding within the framework of a hermeneutic of everyday life, both understanding and reason undergo a transfiguration. Understanding is seen as a precategorial deployment of meaning in the interpretation of self and world. Reason becomes, within this broader scheme of things, a posture of vision and insight, commemoration and foresight, that envelops not only the intentionality of categorial thinking but also the interpretive understanding within the texture of lived experience. What is at issue here is a broadened or expanded notion of reason, more originative than the categorial reason of philosophy and the technological reason of science. Reason as the insight of seeing and acting is as much a resident within the "sight" of praxis as within the project of pure thought or within the calculative thinking of science. This expanded and vitalized notion of reason finds articulation in the intentionality of gestures, the lived-body as a comprehension of the world, the dialogic encounter of selves in conflict and community, the planning that goes on in the sector of public affairs, the ritual and rhetoric of religion, and the work of art. Cézanne, for example, must be defended when he resists the expulsion of the painter from the republic of reason. "The painter interprets . . . the painter is not an imbecile," says Cézanne.[6] The painter does not strip the aesthetical from the working of thought but rather points to the origin of thought. He achieves rationality by thinking with the end of his brush.[7]

We have sought to indicate the character of this expanded operation of reason variously as a kind of "insight," "vision," "commemoration," and "foresight." These various notions themselves carry the weight of certain sedimented denotations and connotations and require continuing clarification through the use of dialectics and indirection. We might begin clarifying our expanded notion of reason by distinguishing insight from argumentation, vision (as unmediated seeing) from categorial schematization, and wisdom from objective, propositional knowledge. Such preliminary elucidations are justified, so long as the dialectic of questioning does not congeal into a logic of opposition. It is not that our critical reposturing of the character of reason entails the expulsion of philosophical argumentation and categorial analysis. Nor does it eliminate the objectifying procedures of scientific experimentation. It is rather that it restores the residency of philosophy and science within the native soil of everyday thought, language, and action.

The chief difficulty in articulating the working of this broadened notion of reason has to do with the elusiveness of the phenomenon at issue. Reason, as it operates in everyday life, is not an entity nor is it a faculty of the soul. It has neither the entitative status of a cosmological principle, which it assumed in the course of the development of Greek metaphysical thought, nor is it an identifiable faculty along the lines of modern epistemologically-oriented reflection. It is more like a "performance" than like an entity or a faculty. Yet the language of performance can slip into a psychologism or an anthropologism if performance is restrictively defined as an *act* or even a competence of a thinking subject. The performing operation of reason antedates the mental act of an epistemological subject. It is at work in the illumination of possibilities already entertained and enacted within the tradition of thought and praxis, as well as in the illumination of possibilities projected against the horizon of the future. Hence, the need to characterize this reason in terms of commemoration and foresight.[8]

Admittedly the performance of reason in philosophical argumentation and categorial analysis does assume the posture of act intentionality which implicates, if not a subject, some notion of a "self" that performs the act. However, what is of concern in our expanded notion of reason is its performative process within the prephilosophical and prescientific praxis of everyday life. On this originary level, the performance of reason is as much the work of the community as it is of any particular self, bearing the inscriptions of social memories and marking out future anticipations. Reason registers its originative demand as a responsibility and task within the thought and praxis of a "community of investigators" (Peirce) and a "community of loyalties" (Royce). Reason bears the inscription of insight and vision, commemoration and foresight, in the association, labor, and communication of everyday life.

One of the more noteworthy implications of our expanded notion of reason for a hermeneutic of everyday life is its bearing on
the phenomena of the nonrational and the irrational. Technical
reason, in the genres of philosophical analysis and scientific calculation, lacks the requisite resources for addressing the relevance of
these ineradicable phenomena in the life of man and society.
These phenomena need to be recognized and explicated because
they appear repeatedly, and sometimes unexpectedly, as ingredients within the formation-process of everyday life. They are
themselves, if you will, world-facts within the general configurative presence of world experience. Hence, their neglect by any
science or philosophy of man results in a sacrifice of adequacy in
accounting for the texture and dynamics of lived experience. In
addressing this issue, we must first clarify the institutionalized use
of the concepts of "nonrational" and "irrational."

Traditionally these concepts have been defined simply as the
negation of the rationality of technical reason in philosophy and
science. The unique contribution of Nietzsche and particularly
Kierkegaard was to register a mistrust of technical reason as the
paradigm of rationality and thus acknowledge the relevance of the
rational and the irrational. Freud was in a position to bring
the importance of a thematic of the irrational to the foreground
from the perspective of the science of psychology and metapsychology, taking recourse to his celebrated theory of the unconscious for an explanation of this pervasive phenomenon.

Although Freud was interested in the irrational principally as a
psychological aberration, his contribution to hermeneutical inquiry was considerable. This contribution can be seen not only on
the metapsychological level, which in Freud's project necessitated
a technique of interpretive understanding whereby the analyst is
able to work his way from the surface manifestations of speech
and behavior to a more primary dynamics of the psyche caught in
the conflict of instinctual urges and repressive norms. The contribution can also be seen within the wider context of hermeneutics
as an experiential form of everyday thought and action. A hermeneutic of everyday life cannot cut itself off from the
phenomena that are disclosed in a "psychopathology of everyday
life." These phenomena are part of the meaning-formation process at work in the structure and dynamics of human life. The
range of norm-governed rationality does not exhaust the determinations of what it means to be human.

The recognition that the nonrational and irrational are themselves formative ingredients within the personal and social development of human life is one of the many considerations that

requires a redefinition of traditional hermeneutical theory. Hermeneutics can no longer rest content with the textual model that governed the various projects of biblical exegesis, inaugurated during the Reformation period and continuing up to the present. Schleiermacher's contribution to hermeneutical theory was still principally along these lines, although he expanded the textual model to include legal documents and extrabiblical literary works. Dilthey further expanded the utility of the textual model and used it in the service of his program of laying the foundations for the humanities and the human sciences.

With the publication of Heidegger's *Being and Time* and Gadamer's *Truth and Method,* a new turn in hermeneutical reflection is effected. Heidegger proposes a "hermeneutic of *Dasein,*" which moves out from an analytic of human existence that is designed to lay out the structures of self-understanding. *Dasein* is itself hermeneutical since it is that being that already understands itself in the preontological comprehension of its everyday concerns. Gadamer proceeds from a Heideggerian standpoint but gives a renewed emphasis to the formation process of the tradition and the role of consciousness as historical understanding.

In our attempted recovery of the texture of everyday life as the proper operational field for interpretive understanding, we are admittedly following a path of inquiry marked out by Heidegger and Gadamer. Requesting the liberty for a metaphorical extension of the meaning of "text" so as to encompass the "texture" of everyday life as a "context" of meaning-formations, we propose a revisionary hermeneutic that continues to be inspired by the pioneering works of Heidegger and Gadamer. Yet, neither Heidegger nor Gadamer have fully grasped the significance of the new hermeneutic for dealing with the irrational. It was precisely on this issue that the limitation of a literary-textual model for hermeneutics became most visible. The irrational remains as a positive feature of the texture of world experience and needs to be comprehended within its developmental process. It is not at all like a textual "error" in a literary corpus that can be set aside as an adventitious intrusion because it has no bearing on the intended meaning of the author. The irrational is not an adventitious intrusion upon the meaning-fabric of man's personal and social existence. Its significance needs to be articulated as part of the context of personal behavior and social goals. This then would seem to require an enlarged notion of reason that goes beyond the reciprocal definition of the irrational by its contraposition to technical reason and the definition of technical reason in terms of its exclusion of the irrational.

One of the more troublesome features of Husserl's very influential notion of the life-world is the question concerning the
source and meaning of reason and its position within the fabric of
the life-world. Werner Marx in *Reason and World* calls our attention to this troublesome feature in his discussion of Husserl's attempt to ground rationality in the freedom of the primordial ego.
"But how is it to be explained," muses Marx, that this primordial
ego "does not make use of its freedom to become nonrational?
Why does it seem to be naturally directed toward rationality?"[9] To
this question posed by Werner Marx, one might attach a rider:
"And what is the peculiar shape and bearing of this rationality?"
Assuredly Husserl became sensitive to these questions as he
moved from the transcendental phenomenological idealism of his
early period to the thematic of the life-world in his later period.
There are indications that the rationality that functions as a *telos* in
the exploration of the life-world is not precisely the same as the
rationality of the primordial ego that is presupposed in the project
of phenomenology as "rigorous science." Husserl seems to exhibit
in his later reflections a more acute awareness of the historical
conditionedness and social sources of rationality than he exhibited
in his earlier program. Yet, that nettle which might unravel the
cord of reason so as to make visible its intricate fabric was not
firmly grasped by Husserl even in his later philosophy. Hence we
still find ourselves in that time of need and existential disquietude
in which, as John O'Neill has so poignantly put it, "reason no
longer seems sure of its own calling."[10]

Reason is no longer, and probably has never been, an unprob-
lematic vocation of man. "What does it mean to be rational?" is a
question that needs to be reopened time and again; and it is a
question that becomes particularly urgent when methodological
and technological rationality seem to be the only candidates on the
slate. The domains of the irrational and the nonrational, as we
have indicated, have been defined by the narrow legislative
criteria of technical, philosophical, and scientific reason, thus setting the requirement for an expanded notion of reason resident
in everyday life. This expanded notion of reason installs the responsibility for a vigilance over the limits of technical reason and
makes possible an interrogation of the significance of the irrational (as the negation of technical reason) in the ongoing process
of a prephilosophical and prescientific comprehension of life and
the world.

The task of fleshing out the notion of reason as an insight and
vision that antedates the split of technical reason and the irrational is a difficult one. In what manner of concretion does this

reason achieve articulation? Where in the folds of everyday personal and public concerns is the presence of this reason manifest? What can be said about the embodiment of this expanded reason? One might profitably at this juncture appeal to the correlation of reason and word, which goes back to the ancient Greeks and which may have been an originative discovery that merits reclamation. Clearly, this correlation has suffered intermittent distortions in the designs of rationalist metaphysics, but this should not preclude the effort to readdress and reformulate the correlation within the context of the current situation of crisis affecting the sciences of man.

It would seem that the contemporary preoccupation with language—by Heideggerians, Wittgensteinians, structuralists, and critical theorists—provides an opportune moment for the revitalization of the connection between reason and word. The later Wittgenstein's adage that language is a "form of life" is by now well known, as is the application of this adage by Peter Winch in his linguistic hermeneutic of language-interpretive social science. Winch's point of departure would seem to have the virtue of retaining a liaison with the actual context of human life, moving out from the mundane truth that both personal and social existence are governed by rules, however loosely these rules may be defined. This rule-governed behavior in everyday personal and public life is linguistically articulated through the spoken word of ordinary communicative performances. The accent is put on the performative character of language as it functions in the interpretive understanding and communication of practical life interests and motivations.

According to Winch, the ramifications of this linguistic approach to rule-governed behavior are consequential for any social science. "What the sociologist is studying, as well as his study of it," says Winch, "is a human activity and is therefore carried on according to rules."[11] Social science must thus look in the direction of the linguistic rules which inform our ordinary discourse for an understanding of social phenomena, i.e., human motives and actions. Socio-historical explanation, according to Winch, "is not the application of generalizations and theories to particular instances: it is the tracing of internal relations. It is like applying one's knowledge of a language in order to understand a conversation rather than like applying one's knowledge of the laws of mechanics to understand the workings of a watch."[12] The understanding of social phenomena, in Winch's linguistic hermeneutic, does not proceed via a subsumption of particular motives, actions, and events under a general law so as to explain the law-like character of these particulars in reference to their antecedent conditions. Hence, the general law model, with its presupposed detached objectivity and nomothetic procedures, falls under indictment.

In all this we can discern not only a critique of positivistic science but also a broader critical framework in which the classical Enlightenment concept of reason, with its drive toward a universal rationalistic worldview, is brought under critical scrutiny. Winch seeks to rescue the sciences of man from objectifying methodological distortions so as to reclaim their originary data. The distinctive function of the social sciences becomes that of an interrogation of rule-informed motives and actions as these occur in the actual context of daily life. The meaning of social facts involving agents and their actions is apprehended through an interpretive understanding of the way in which the active subject lives his particular style of life. This requires on the part of the investigator, the social scientist, a participative understanding of the intentions of the agents and the patterns of the social life that are being observed. The detached objectivity and the construction of general laws, which remain the ideals of positivistic social science, give way to a linguistically oriented hermeneutic of everyday life.

There is much that remains plausible in Winch's language-interpretive social science. His critique of the nomothetic models of positivistic reductionism is careful and consequential, and his appeal to the rule-governed meanings of ordinary language usage provides a possible springboard for a hermeneutic of everyday life. Yet, certain critical adjustments in his approach would need to be made. These adjustments move in the direction of an extension of his linguistic hermeneutic so as to provide a more expansive epistemological space for the ongoing process of meaning-formation. Linguistic hermeneutics needs to be incorporated into a more originary context of cultural hermeneutics. Such a revisionism might be accomplished by working through two related problems in Winch's language-interpretive programmatic.

The first problem concerns the source and status of the rules that allegedly govern human behavior. According to Winch, and one might say linguistic philosophers more generally, linguistic rules govern the meaning of the motives, decisions, and actions of social subjects. In short, rules confer meaning on social action and interaction and account for the orderedness of the social order. Through an understanding and interpretation of these rules, social processes and events become intelligible.

A troublesome feature of this inquiry framework is that it invites a *rule a priorism* that fails to account for the genesis of rule-informed meaning within the fabric of social thought and action. Ernest Gellner points to the critical issue at hand when he says: "The constraints, the rules within which social life is played out, are themselves a *consequence* [italics mine] of the game."[13] According to Gellner, rules are the *result* rather than the antecedent conditions of the upsurge of meaning in the social order. Now it may be that Gellner's critical rejoinder to Winch overreaches its target and conceals the formative contribution of rules within the genealogy and development of social behavior. It would appear that there is more of a consummate reciprocity between linguistic rules and social behavior than either Winch or Gellner would seem to acknowledge. Contra Winch, it must be said that we do not understand the rules that govern human behavior prior to the study of behavior itself; contra Gellner, it must be said that rules are ingredients rather than simple consequences of the game of social life as it is being played out. Instead of constructing a framework of antecedent and consequent determinations, we would propose a framework of dialectical interdependence and interplay. In studying the life of a society, we do not know the rules prior to the events of social behavior nor is the behavior known prior to the rules. The model of serial determination, causal or otherwise, is peculiarly limited for an inquiry into the reciprocity of linguistic rules and social behavior in the ongoing process of social formation. Linguistic rules do indeed inform the constellations of meaning in the variant motives, actions, and roles that are played out in the social world; but also it should be recognized that developing social roles and revolutionary social change conspire to produce modifications in the registry of rules.[14]

A language-interpretive social science, of the sort proposed by Winch, is thus unavoidably limited in its hermeneutical task. Its interpretive format needs to be extended so as to provide a more inclusive context for the interplay between language and social reality. This more inclusive context is history, in the originative signification of the term, understood as the story of the personal and social life of man. The question of the "science" of history, as distinct from a possible "science" of nature, is not yet at issue here. What is at issue is history as the context of the text of everyday life. The text of everyday life, with its communicative operations in which linguistic rules are constantly put into play but are also subject to modification in the evolutions and revolutions of social change, needs to be reinserted into the context of historical experience. This framework of reflection to a great extent has been opened up by the seminal explorations of Gadamer. Gadamer has

sought to reconstitute hermeneutics as a project of cultural interpretation which proceeds neither from an interrogation of the
subjective contents residing in the intentions of the social agents
nor from the objectified contents of man's institutional achievements, but from the creative process of a "historically operating
consciousness" (*Wirkungsgeschichtliches Bewusstsein*).[15] The system of
interpretive rules appealed to by the human scientist in his attempt to understand human thought and action is reintegrated
into the tradition of man's historical existence, and no longer
functions simply as a logical precondition for an understanding of
human behavior.[16] In this recognition of the historical and
tradition-imbued context of linguistic rules, we are able at the
same time to surmount the Winchean problem of failing to account for the genesis and dialectical development of rules and
avoid the a priori exclusion of the *sense* of tradition in the restricted concept of reason that issued from the Enlightenment and
subsequent developments of positivism.

The second and related problem that rears its head in the
language-interpretive social science proposed by Winch, and
which provides further warrant for an extension of his linguistic
hermeneutic, is the virtual identification of rationality with rule-
governed behavior and the consequent exclusion of significations
attaching to the repression of rational motivation. The principal
task of the social scientist, according to Winch, is to understand
the agent or social subject as he endows his motives and actions
with meaning in accordance with rule-governed, linguistic rationality. What is neglected in such a definition of the hermeneutical
project is an attentiveness to the recurring suspension of the rules
and the consequences of this for the configurative development of
the socio-historical life of man. There are segments of both personal and social life that remain "irrational" in the sense that rational motivation is repressed. Human behavior does not always
follow the path of an endowment of meaning through rule-
governed linguistic performance. The rationality of motives,
which according to Winch becomes the phenomenon to be interpreted by the social scientist, is sometimes simply absent. Thus a
hermeneutical model which restricts itself to an understanding of
the agent's linguistic rationality remains partial at best and misleading at worst. Misleading interpretations are particularly prone
to occur within such an approach when the social scientist imputes
his culture-bound and rule-governed criteria of rational action to
an observed agent in an alien culture in an effort to render his
action intelligible.

If the agent's linguistically conditioned reasons for his behavior no longer comprise the sole object or goal of social science inquiry, then the scope of hermeneutical understanding needs to be expanded. We need to ask not only about the linguistic, rule-governed rationality of the agent—we assuredly need to do this—but we also need to ask about the conditions under which repression of rational motivation might occur (Freud), conditions under which social factors amalgamate so as to introduce ideological illusions (Marx), and the conditions under which people become subject to the duplicity of bad-faith or self-deception (Sartre). It is thus that the rule-governed, language-interpretive social science of Winch needs to be enlarged so as to make possible an articulation of the bearing of the nonrational and the irrational on the project of self and cultural understanding. Again, we are led to inquire about an expanded notion of reason, encompassing the formative process of a historical tradition in which not only certain linguistic rules of ordinary discourse and communication are operative but also the recurrence of repressive conditions of rational motivation, the presence of ideological illusions, and the insinuation of self-deception in its multiple expressions. Now it is precisely this connection of reason and history that we must address and clarify.

The question of the rationality of everyday life and the project of an interpretive understanding of this everyday life as it deals with the origin of the sciences of man has now found its proper context. History provides the context for the text of everyday life. Above we have recommended an enlarged notion of reason, distinguishing it from the concept of technical reason that provided the criterion for deciding on that which is "irrational" and "nonrational." In this decision the *significance* of the irrational and nonrational for everyday life was denied because the reach and range of the significant was predefined by the fiat of technical reason. It is surely not surprising that such a restriction of the meaning of reason and such a limitation on the range of signification should be accompanied by a negative view of the historical tradition. In the classical Enlightenment concept of reason, which already defined the direction of the current technical view of reason, tradition itself was placed outside the domain of the rational. The Enlightenment ideal of reason came into its own through an alleged liberation from all tradition and authority. Contextless and objectivistic, reason was to recognize no authority but itself. In its philosophical expression, the Enlightment concept of reason sought its foundations in an isolated epistemological subject; in its socio-political expression, it made its appearance in a declaration of the individual rights of a radically individualized rational man, liberated from the sanctions of all governmental and ecclesiastical institutions. Cut off from tradition, the Enlightenment model of reason, and its further narrowing in contemporary philosophical positivism, assumed the stance of a detached objectivity.

The articulation of reason as the performance of commemoration and foresight, vision and thought, enables us to restore the context of tradition and the significance of the historical for the formation of meaning in the warp and woof of everyday life. This broadened perspective contributes a needed corrective to the methodological and metaphysical individualism which has from time to time infected both the philosophy and science of man. The process of meaning-formation that is at work in the speech, thought, and action of everyday life, and which it is the task of the human sciences to disclose in their varied partitive profiles, is not the isolated achievement of an encapsulated subject endowing his behavior with meaning. The agent or actor comports his life with meanings that are already delivered over from his historical tradition. It is relative to this consideration that Merleau-Ponty's ruminations "We are condemned to meaning"[17] and "The transcendental descends into history"[18] take on a peculiar ontological weight. The meanings that the social subject expresses in his motivations and with which he endows his actions are not simply authored by the individual subject. They bear the coauthorship of the individual and his historical tradition. This truth of man's historicity, forgotten in Sartre's dictum "We are condemned to freedom" is recalled in Merleau-Ponty's reformulation "We are condemned to meaning." For Sartre, meaning is the creation of a resolute *pour soi*, exercising its radical freedom. For Merleau-Ponty, meaning is already installed in the life-world by virtue of a milieu and a tradition; and in this life-world, the self-understanding of the social subject appropriates the influx of meaning from the historical past. In apprehending that we are "condemned to meaning," we thus concomittantly grasp the truth of the descent of the transcendental into history.

In the literature on the human sciences, it has become fashionable, almost to the point of becoming a mark of the trade, to formulate topics in terms of the alliterative dilemmas of self vs. society, consciousness vs. the collective, individuals vs. institutions, and persons vs. the public. Upon critical scrutiny, however, these dichotomies reduce to a hollow and abstract artificiality. In part they are the result of an endemic professionalism that infects the republic of the human sciences, producing a situation in which the psychological, the sociological, and the historical sciences of man stake out claims for disciplined studies of the individual, the social, and the historical in such a manner that each arrogates to itself a special privilege. On a more fundamental level, however, these artificial dilemmas can be seen as the natural consequence of that epistemology of pure theory and abstracted empiricism of which we have provided a radical critique in the two preceding chapters. A relocation of the process of meaning-establishment within the stream of everyday life and an attentiveness to the requirement of a reflexivity on the part of philosophy and the human sciences, whereby the path of return to the origin is kept open, should do much to avoid the artificial problem construction of pure theory and abstracted empiricism alike. What becomes urgent, however, for any hermeneutic of everyday life that seeks to restore the context of history is an explication of the symbiosis of thought and praxis in the developing tradition of human culture, and a specification of the performative role of reason in this development.[19]

To apprehend the ingression of the historical tradition into the ongoing process of everyday life, it is crucial that one achieve clarity as to the question with which to address the phenomenon. Given the varied senses of "history" and "historical," it is mandatory that a hermeneutic of everyday life mark out its path of inquiry with some care. Neither the analytical-methodological approach to the philosophy of history nor the speculative-substantive approach is under consideration here. Indeed, the categorial framework of a "philosophy of history" is precisely that which needs to be overcome. The pivotal question that addresses the workings of the historical tradition is neither the analytical-methodological question "In what sense is the study of history a science?" nor the speculative-substantive question, "What is the nature of the historical process itself?" but rather the hermeneutical-interpretive question "How does the participant in everyday life appropriate and understand the historical inscriptions within his experienced world?" The principal topic is neither the logic of historical inquiry nor the schematization of an objective essence of world history, but rather an interrogation of the sense of tradition as it is *lived-through*. What needs to be highlighted is the experience of the historical as the story of our personal and social existence in its configurative character of concreteness and functioning intentionality. It is this quality of "living-through" that indicates the hallmark of experiencing something. Hence the lead question interrogating the context of the tradition that surrounds everyday life can be posed as the question concerning the *experience* of the historical.[20] The term "experience," here as elsewhere, must not be confused with the epistemological use of

this term within an abstracted empiricism. It is meant to indicate
the concrete unity of insight and action that pervades the in-
volvements and concerns of everyday life. Experience, properly
understood, retains both the aspect of seeing into a situation and
acting within it, which are constitutive aspects of every concrete
occasion of self-understanding. As such, the notion of experience
is much preferable over the notion of consciousness, which has
from the beginning informed a variety of idealist approaches to
history. The limitation of the concept of "historical consciousness"
is that it fails to designate the reciprocity of insight and action,
thought and praxis and, thus, invites the view that history is in
some way the manifestation of mind.[21]

The historical as a feature of the experienced life-world registers its significations by delivering a world of predecessors. Tradition insinuates itself into the text of everyday life through a
matrix of social memories. The weight of tradition, which the
Enlightenment concept of reason sought to suppress, leaves its
inscriptions on the language, the thought, and the praxis of
everyday life. The motives and actions of contemporaries are sur-
rounded with the fringes of a historical past which continue to
impinge on the present. Man as social agent, in his communication and planning, may indeed be the maker of the world of to-
morrow; but he is also the receiver of a tradition. Now it is
precisely this *reception* of a tradition that needs to be clarified. We
have remarked above that the tradition insinuates itself into the
everyday life of contemporary man through a complex of delivered social memories. This is indeed the first observation that
needs to be made. Common memories conspire to bestow meaning on the present spoken word, on current constellations of
praxis, and on future anticipations which are projected from the
here and now. Yet, it would appear that the thread of memory,
individual and collective, is too fragile to secure the deliverance of
the past. The tradition comprises not only that which is consciously remembered, but also a plethora of unconscious motivations, ideologies whose source has been forgotten, and hidden
processes of self-deception—all of which are at work in the tradition and continue to shape the significance of the present for its
bearers and receivers. Forgotten events direct deliberations on
socio-political planning, forgotten language exerts its influence in
the linguistic operations of everyday communication, and a forgotten sense of being infects the project of human self-
understanding.[22] Hence, there is a demand for a broadened notion of reason as a performing operation, so as to retain the relevance of the forgotten and the concealed for the ongoing process

of everyday life. The intentionality of the memory of technical reason is too frail to deliver the significations of the forgotten, the opaque, the concealed, the suppressed, and the irrational.

At this juncture, the failures of most modern approaches to the philosophy of history become evident. The idealist approach in particular, which has dominated modern and contemporary philosophies of history from Hegel to Collingwood, has construed history as the history of thought. The bearer of history, thusly understood, is historical consciousness, striving to reenact the thought of the past. Within such a scheme of analysis there is first of all a failure to recognize the contribution by the praxis of historical groups to the patterns of meaning within personal and social existence. Idealism, even in its more attenuated varieties, tends to diminish the dimension of praxis because of its disposition towards a perspective of pure theory. If there is to be any talk of a reenactment of the past in the project of historical understanding, this reenactment needs to comport the influx of the significations of praxis, which remain submerged in the abstractions of pure reflective thought. It is also this abstract and technical rationality that underlies the idealistic requirement for a coincidence of past and present as the condition for historical understanding. Technical reason, both in its speculative and analytical expression, is uncomfortable with the phenomenon of temporal becoming. For the most part, it considers time as an intruder. It yearns for the constancy of an epistemological space that determines the ordination of significations in terms of the fixity of class concepts or a self-evidence present for consciousness.

Applied to an understanding of history, such an epistemic model requires the coincidence of the past with the present as a condition for its being known. Reason as a performance within the cultural life of man, not yet severed from the ongoing temporal stream of human experience, is able to assume a more positive attitude toward the past. It allows for a recognition of the "distance" of the past from the present and the function of distantiation in the project of interpretive understanding. The past as distanced from the present is considered not as an epistemological negativity to be overcome but rather as the region for a hermeneutical reclamation of significations which were once extant and continue to exert an influence on the present. The significance of the past is apprehended vis-à-vis its bearing on the present without being reduced to the epistemic conditions of an actualized present. The past is, if you will, perpetually translated into a possibility for further determinations of meaning. Its significance is never exhausted as a completed, classificatory state of affairs. Reason as performative insight perpetually opens the past to new perspectives of meaning.

Not only does the paradigmatic use of technical reason, either in the services of a speculative or analytical philosophy of history, submerge the formative role of praxis within historical groups and epistemologically restrict the understanding of the past, it also fails to comprehend the significations of the forgotten, the suppressed, and the irrational for an understanding of the texture of everyday life. The latter, as we have already seen, is a peculiar limitation of Winch's rule-governed linguistic hermeneutic as applied to the study of social reality. Neither the resources of a linguistic, rule-governed rationality nor the technical epistemological reason of a remembering subject of consciousness are able to deliver the significance of the past as it shapes the meaning of the present. An enlarged notion of reason is required. But the pivotal feature in the demand for an enlarging of reason, as it pertains to a hermeneutic of everyday existence, has not yet been thematically isolated. This pivotal feature has to do with the *language* of reason, and more specifically with the recognition that the language of expanded reason has an indelible mytho-poetic component.

One of the more pressing demands of a hermeneutic of everyday life is to retrieve the thought and praxis of the world of predecessors as it impinges on the world of contemporaries through a discernment of the role played by myth and symbol. In the deliverance of the tradition, the language of myth and symbol performs a decisive disclosing or revelatory function. The thought and praxis of the tradition is articulated not only through its historiological reports but also through its myths, legends, sagas, and epic poetry. The tradition that surrounds and contextualizes everyday life unites scientific-historical reports with mytho-symbolic interpretation. The *logos* of scientific-technical reason blends with the *logos* of *mythos*.[23] Reason, in its broadened signification, speaks both in the language of science and the language of myth. The contribution of this expanded reason is not that it reduces science to myth but that it salvages the *logos* present in myth. A prejudice has long existed both in philosophy and the human sciences against any knowledge claims by *mythos* and *poesis*. The Enlightenment concept of reason, in its various forms of apostolic succession, found it necessary, because of its restrictive character, to expunge myth from the domain of rational consciousness. Certain historically influential anthropologists, notably Tylor, Frazer, Durkheim, and Lévy-Bruhl, brought to their studies of myth an evolutionary model whereby myth was prejudged as a relic of primitive societies which was superseded by the development of man's rational consciousness and the introduction of logico-scientific modes of thought.

Only in recent times has a more positive assessment of the role of the mytho-poetic in the cultural life of man been propounded. This turn of events has been discernible in philosophy (Ricoeur), anthropology and sociology (Lévi-Strauss), psychology (Freud and Jung), political theory (Cassirer), theology (Tillich), and the history of religion (Eliade). This is not to say that the representatives of these disciplines speak about myth with a common mind, but they all recognize that mythic consciousness is a constitutive feature of the story of man in all stages of his socio-historical development. They no longer see myth as a prescientific distortion of the thought of primitive man. The mytho-poetic is viewed as an ingredient within the thought and praxis by which men in all ages live.[24]

Freud's contribution to the relevance of myth for the human sciences, and especially psychology and psychoanalysis, although controversial, has been remarkably influential. His psychoanalytical hermeneutic underlying his interpretation of dreams and his "psychopathology of everyday life" forced the science of psychology to recognize the importance of myth as an articulation of the formative influence of the irrational in the cultural life of man. What Freud did not provide is a metapsychoanalytical interpretive stance for the comprehension of the mytho-poetic as it relates to the wider communicative and praxis-oriented projects of human existence. The reason why such a metapsychoanalytic framework of interpretation is not forthcoming in Freud is principally due to a blockage residing in his psychoanalytical theory construction. In his effort to provide a theoretical foundation for his psychoanalytical procedures, Freud was disposed to appeal solely to the criteriology of technical reason in designing the theoretical foundations. There is thus a shift from the pragmatics of psychoanalytical procedure to the theory of scientific explanation. In this shift the *logos* of myth suffers a reduction to the *logos* of technical reason. Myth undergoes what Ricoeur has so aptly characterized as a process of "demystification."[25] The significations of myth are translated into objective scientific truths about the nature of the human psyche.

A similar process of demystification is discernible in Lévi-Strauss's structural analysis of myth. In Lévi-Strauss's structuralism, myth is shorn of its extrascientific signification through the employment of a logic of classification that proceeds in terms of a linguistic model of binary opposition and a truth-functional paradigm of class inclusion and exclusion. On the infrastructure level, all myths exhibit a logico-linguistic model, which the ethnographer brings with himself as he seeks to collate and interpret the empirical data from the native culture in which the myth arose. Although Lévi-Strauss recognizes, contra the proponents of the evolutionary theory, that myth is a constitutive feature in the life of all societies past and present, he never proceeds beyond the technical-scientific rationality of the Enlightenment concept of reason. Like Freud, he carries through his own project of myth demystification.

The required and difficult task of myth interpretation is that of proceeding in such a manner that reference to the concrete multivalence of significations in the lived historical understanding is not lost. When it becomes a matter of hermeneutical method, myth interpretation is an interpretation of interpretations. Within the originary matrix of lived experience, a precategorial understanding of self and world infused by mytho-poetic interpretation is already operative. Any philosophy or science of man has the responsibility of fashioning its methodological procedures in such a manner as to allow the originary ongoing process of mytho-poetic self-understanding to show itself. The methodological procedure employed should move out from and return to that originary, ongoing process of interpretation which unfolds in the thought and praxis of lived experience. It is on this originative level that the mytho-poetic first registers its concrete multivalence of significations. Merleau-Ponty points us in this direction when he says, "The myth holds the essence *within* the appearance; the mythical phenomenon is not a representation, but a genuine presence."[26] The sinews of mytho-poetic meaning-formation are not located behind the appearances, requiring for their visibility a categorial apprehension of a set of relations and ideas that are veiled by the language of myth; they are embedded in the myth's manner of appearing. The meaning of myth is not the achievement of a representation mediated by an objectifying concept, but rather the *logos* incarnated in the experience of presence as the fulfilled moment of vison and action. Thus Ricouer is able to say that any hermeneutic of myth must be geared in the direction of "the recollection of meaning and reminiscence of being."[27] The mytho-poetic is here approached not as a blade that severs the source of meaning, and much less as a distortion, but rather as a genuine message which announces the concrescence that determines the experience of presence, into which are gathered a multidimensionality of social, political, psychological, moral, artistic, and religious significations. This presence of multivalent significations, it needs to be underscored, is noncontrolled and nondeliberative. The life of myth is not consciously engineered by the controlling technical reason of a subject of consciousness. Myths are not the achievements of a reflective consciousness. The inscriptions of myth are older than the biography of the consciousness of an epistemological subject.

Because of this concrete multivalence of significations in the life of myth antedating the constructs of technical reason, any traditional epistemology of myth is destined for disappointment. Epistemology, as it has developed particularly in modern philosophy, has stood in the service of either an analytical or a speculative technical reason that has been shaped by the transcendental-empirical doublet and its various positionings of transcendental and empirical consciousness. The language and intentionality of the mytho-poetic bring into sharp relief the limits of technical reason in deciphering the patterns of meaning in the ongoing process of everyday life, particularly as these patterns take shape as the recollection of the tradition in the experience of the streaming present. Mytho-poetic meaning is neither the achievement of the categorial constitution of a transcendental ego, nor the result of an empirical description of a state of affairs. Thus we now see how our radicalization of knowledge in chapter 3, whereby the transcendental-empirical framework of inquiry is overcome, places the project of myth interpretation beyond the methods and designs of formal epistemology.

Similar considerations require the placing of myth interpretation beyond the methods and designs of any formal linguistics of myth. The science of linguistics must of necessity approach language as an object. This objectification of language by linguistic science is unavoidable and retains its own legitimacy. Objectification, as Marx had already discerned, is not in itself alienation. The science of linguistics should be spared the charge that it entails an intrinsic falsification or distortion of language. Phonemics, phonology, morphology, syntactics, and semantics require for their success the objectification of phonemes, morphemes, grammatical forms, and relations of reference. The subject-object framework of inquiry remains normative for linguistic science. But as the subject-object framework of inquiry in epistemology needs to be overcome through a process of deconstruction so as to render visible a more originative posturing of thought, so also the subject-object framework of inquiry in the science of linguistics needs to be overcome so as to bring to light a more originative, preobjective experience of language. The phenomenon of myth provides us with a dramatic example of the simultaneous disclosure of preobjective thought and preobjective language, which then mandates the responsibility for a reflexivity on the origin of epistemology and linguistics as formal disciplines. The self and world understanding within mytho-poetic language requires considerations that go beyond the structural elements, grammatical forms, and syntactical rules of linguistic science. The signs and symbols of mytho-poetic language conspire in a genesis and giving of meanings as they develop in the fabric of everyday, socio-historical existence. These meanings are simply not reducible to the criteria of objectifying thought and language. Here the disclosing function of language takes precedence over its representational function. Language no longer functions simply as the representation of ideas and relations nor as the transmission of information as a commodity. It is experienced as the *lumen naturale* of the praxis of a tradition that vitalizes and informs the historical presence of everyday thought and action.

But if every epistemology of myth and every linguistics of myth is destined for disappointment, how can myth become a legitimate subject of inquiry for a philosophy or a science of man? Indeed how can philosophy and the sciences of man study myth without disturbing the concrete multivalence of significations inscribed on everyday praxis? Are we placed into the position of proclaiming a "hands-off policy" for the sciences of man when it comes to matters of myth? Are we to section off the domain of myth as a region of pure and untrammeled prephilosophical and prescientific *sui generis* insights so as to keep them untarnished by philosophical reflection and scientific explanation? If this is the case, this would surely produce a distressing state of affairs for any philosophy or science of man. If the sciences of man are indeed to provide knowledge about that which is human, and if the mytho-poetic affords an experiential comprehension of the concrete significations of the socio-historical life of man, then the human sciences cannot shirk the responsibility of assuming some kind of cognitive attitude toward the phenomenon of myth. It was the genius of Lévi-Strauss to recognize this, but it also was a most grevious fault of his to construe the *logos* of myth as a nascent objective science, amenable to a system of classification based on a logic of opposition. Lévi-Strauss's application of structuralist techniques in the study of myth leads to a reduction of the contents of myth to the representational language of science as it is informed by technical reason.

But if the human sciences have a responsibility to take into account the role of the phenomenon of myth in an understanding of human behavior and the broader developments in the cultural life of man, and if they are correspondingly enjoined to desist from any reduction of myth to the representational language of science informed by technical reason, are they not saddled with a paradoxical task? This may be the case; however, a paradoxical task is not necessarily an impossible one. Assuredly any philosophy or science of man must employ the logic of technical reason. In the case of the human science, as in all sciences, rational explanation and objectifying procedures are integral features of their methods and designs.

The human sciences cannot be asked to suspend the use of technical reason. The requirement is neither to displace technical reason nor to develop a poetic conception of science. Some of the more antinomian representatives of existentialism have moved in the former direction; Foucault, in his bold and encompassing reinterpretation of the sciences of man, has moved in the latter direction.[28] Admittedly the human sciences, as well as philosophical anthropology, can no longer follow the ideal of reason as it had been shaped by the Enlightenment and later by positivism. The absolute sovereignty of technical reason needs to be contested. But the proper response to this idolatry of technique and objectivity is not a suppression but rather a reposturing of the role and range of technical reason within the context of life's demands and solicitations. Our general requirement for a reflexivity on the part of the sciences of man now receives more specific expression in the demand for an epistemic self-reflexivity of technical reason in search of its field of origin, in which it will find a broader notion of reason at work, encompassing not only the *logos* of science and formal philosophy but also the *logos* of myth. The role of radical reflection is precisely that of disclosing this field of origin and announcing the requirement of reflexivity.

It is against this background of the field of origin, uncovered by radical reflection, that the paradoxical attitude of the sciences of man to the mytho-poetic must be articulated. Reflexive upon an origin which is prephilosophical and prescientific and which bears the inscriptions of the mytho-poetic, the human sciences must remain scientific in their effort to develop a science of that which is human. The paradox resides, if you will, in the very locution "a science of man." This paradox cannot be dissolved. It cannot be dissolved through the reduction of man to the contingent facts of an abstracted empiricism and a translation of the nonobjectivating language of myth into the representational language of science, nor can it be dissolved through Foucault's proposed translation of scientific prose into poetry. The requirement presented to the human sciences is not that of displacing science and philosophy by myth but rather that of allowing the prethematic significations of the mytho-poetic to play their role in the process of self-understanding within the socio-historical existence of man.

As sciences, the sciences of man need to thematize and objectify, thus making use of technical and analytical reason. This cognitive attitude, inclined toward the thematic and the objective, occasions the thematic constitution of various partitive profiles of the ongoing stream of world experience. The originary matrix of concrete social-historical experience is objectified in such a manner that a particular profile or perspective of it is made to "stand over against" the investigator and is presented as an analyzable thematic field. It is thus, as we have seen, that the various portraits of man, such as "*homo sociologicus*," "*homo politicus*," "*homo oeconomicus*," and "psychological man," are constituted. These portraits, although thematic conceptual constructs, do not by necessity occlude the originary experience of the life-world. If the temptations of abstracted empiricism and reified intellectualism are avoided, objectification and thematization do not as such entail a loss of the phenomena. The use of technical reason on the part of the human sciences need not prejudice the concresence of meaning in everyday life, so long as the broader parameters of the *logos* are observed.

In its thematic constitution of psychic life, psychology will need to render some account of the formative role of myth in psychological self-understanding; and it will need to make use of analytical reason in rendering such an account. Freud has provided us with a classic example of a psychological interpretation of the Greek myth of Oedipus, which yields certain psychoanalytical insights pertaining to the phenomena of latent hostility, repression, guilt feelings, and sublimation. The oedipal myth in Freud's hermeneutic is thematized and objectified in accordance with the method and design of his psychoanalytical theory and practice. The myth is read and interpreted from the perspective of its power to disclose certain psychological truths about the psychopathology of everyday life as well as extreme situations of psychotic behavior. Freud selects a particular myth from the massive corpus of mythology that informed the tradition of praxis and thought of ancient Greece and seeks to wrest from it its psychological meaning. But myths also comport a significance for the everyday self-understanding of social life. The mytho-poetic is part of the process of meaning-formation in the definition of social roles and in the fabric of man's social life more generally. Not only is myth contributory to a "psychopathology of everyday life," it is also an ingredient in a "sociology of everyday life." When Lévi-Strauss carries through an interpretation of the Bororo myths of South America so as to uncover a polarization of nature and culture, we see an illustration of the thematization of myth relative to its social function. Now there is also a more explicit political dimension in the mytho-poetic tradition of praxis, making possible a political thematization of myth. It is here that the mythical element of "Fortune," for example, plays a rather important role, as Cassirer has so incisively demonstrated in his essay *The Myth of the State*.[29] Again, we find an interest in the religious dimension of myth and an attempt to discern how myth functions in an ethico-religious comprehension of the world. Tillich's interpretation of the biblical myth of the Fall of Man, through which he provides a theological perspective on the experience of sin and guilt, affords an example of the theological function of myth.

The foregoing projects of distilling the psychological, sociological, political, and theological meanings of myth illustrate the concrete multivalence of significations that lay embedded in myth and show how the *logos* of *mythos* overflows the perspectival thematizations of any particular human science. In this is an implied regulative principle for any science, philosophy, or theology of man. It is the principle of the avoidance of reductionism, which undercuts any aspiration towards an idolatric epistemic privilege in any single perspective on man. This perspectivity of interpretation by the several disciplined studies of man calls attention to the paradoxical use of a technical-analytical reason, required in the service of thematization and objectification, which drives to its own limits in the recognition of the prethematic constellation of mythic meaning within the originary flow of lived experience. Called upon to perform a thematic and methodic interpretation of an ongoing process of already installed self and social interpretation in everyday life, the human sciences are confronted time and again with the requirement for a reflexivity upon their origin. This requirement makes a critical evaluation of the success and adequacy of the various projects of myth thematization possible. It is then that we are able, for example, to critique Freud's metapsychology of demystification and Lévi-Strauss's structural linguistic objectivism because of their occlusion of certain dimensions of originary mythic signification. This is not to deny or devalue the projects of psychological and sociological myth thematization as such; it is only to place these projects within the context of an expanded notion of reason and a broadened matrix of interpretive understanding.

In this concluding chapter, we have followed the path of radical reflection to an expanded and originary rationality of everyday life that is older than technical reason. This expanded notion of

reason has provided the parameters for a hermeneutic of everyday existence from which every philosophy and science of man
proceeds, either tacitly or explicitly. Reason as the performance of
vision and insight, commemoration and foresight, occasions the
recognition of a process of meaning-formation that gathers within
it the logic of technical reason and the *logos* of myth. In its critical
function, this expanded notion of reason announces the limits of
the technical reason of science and philosophy and provides a
sheet-anchor against its self-elevation to ultimacy. It insures
against the pretension and misuse of rationality in an abstract intellectualism and an abstract empiricism which sever themselves
from the tradition of praxis and its historical genesis of meaning.
In its more positive function, this expanded notion of reason allows the disclosure of a precategorial self-understanding within
the drama of everyday life in which human agents, always in
transit, endow their perceptions and actions with meaning as they
respond to their past and anticipate their future. It makes possible
the search for the significations of the irrational, the ideological,
and self-deception, for they too shape the course of everyday life.
This expanded posture of reason comports within it the *logos* of
myth and enjoins the reflection of philosophy and inquiry of science to be attentive to its concrete multivalent significations.

Our discussion throughout has been offered as an exemplification of radical reflection. Through the practice of radical reflection, we have sought to restore that common center or origin
from which philosophical inquiry and scientific investigation on
the being and behavior of man proceed. The question of the unity
of the sciences of man has been recast into a question of origin.
What is attained in the pursuit of this question is not a common
manual of procedures for the several human sciences, much less a
universal science or a perennial philosophy, but rather a return to
a prescientific and prephilosophical manner of seeing self and
world. Radical reflection drives to the extremities of philosophy
itself and delivers philosophy from the temptation to arrogate to
itself the custodial rights to a final foundation for the special sciences of man. Radical reflection deconstructs the layers of
methodological and metaphysical conceptualization that surround
man's inquiries about himself and his world so as to reopen the
text of everyday life and make visible its language, thought, and
praxis. This text, unlike the text of a literary document in which
the last sentence has to be written and whose pages have to be
bound, remains a living text that is open at both ends. The speech
and the actions of the characters of this original text outstrip the
demarcations of a first and final chapter. The challenge of any

scientific and philosophical study of man, in its aspirations to understand man and his world, is to maintain a reflexivity on this original text.

NOTES

1. A well-informed and systematic review of this literature has been provided by Richard Palmer in his book *Hermeneutics* (Evanston: Northwestern University Press, 1969).

2. *"Die Natur erklären wir, das Seelenleben verstehen wir," Gesammelte Schriften,* Vol. 5: *Die Geistige Welt* (Stuttgart: B.G. Teubner, 1957), p. 144.

3. *Grundriss der Sozialökonomik, III. Abteilung: Wirtschaft und Gesellschaft,* 2nd edition (Tübingen: J.C.B. Mohr, 1925), pp. 3–4.

4. *The Phenomenology of the Social World,* trans. George Walsh and Frederick Lehnert (Evanston: Northwestern University Press, 1967), p. 30.

5. Quoted by Heidegger in his book *Die Kategorien und Bedeutungslehre des Duns Scotus* (Tübingen: Mohr Verlag, 1915), p. 9.

6. Quoted by Merleau-Ponty in his essay, "Cézanne's Doubt," *Sense and Non-Sense,* trans. Hubert Dreyfus and Patricia Dreyfus (Evanston: Northwestern University Press, 1964), p. 15.

7. Merleau-Ponty expresses it well when he says: "Cézanne did not think he had to choose between feeling and thought, between order and chaos. He did not want to separate the stable things which we see and the shifting way in which they appear; he wanted to depict matter as it takes on form, the birth of order through spontaneous organization," *Sense and Non-Sense,* p. 13.

8. Heidegger approaches the commemorative dimension of reason in his interpretation of thinking (*Denken*) as "thinking that recalls" (*Andenken*). See his introduction to the fifth printing of *What is Metaphysics?*, bearing the title "The Way Back into the Ground of Metaphysics," trans. W. Kaufmann, *Existentialism from Dostoevsky to Sartre* (New York: Meridian Books, 1956). However, Heidegger nowhere in his writings works out the relevance of his existentialist ontology, nor his later reflections on thought and language, for the developing human sciences.

9. *Reason and World* (The Hague: Martinus Nijhoff, 1971), p. 56.

10. *Sociology as a Skin Trade: Essays Towards a Reflexive Sociology* (New York: Harper Torchbooks, 1972), p. 14.

128   RADICAL REFLECTION

11. *The Idea of a Social Science* (New York: Humanities Press, 1958), p. 87.

12. *The Idea of a Social Science*, p. 133.

13. Quoted by Thomas Luckmann in *Phenomenology and the Social Sciences*, Vol. 1, ed. Maurice Natanson (Evanston: Northwestern University Press, 1973), p. 176n.

14. For an incisive discussion of this particular issue the reader is referred to William L. McBride, *Fundamental Change in Law and Society: Hart and Sartre on Revolution* (The Hague: Mouton, 1970), and specifically chapter seven of this work, "Rules," pp. 74–83. Also see Karl-Otto Apel, "The Problem of Philosophical Fundamental-Grounding in Light of a Transcendental Pragmatic of Language," *Man and World*, Vol. 8, No. 3, 1975.

15. See particularly his discussion in the section, *"Das Prinzip der Wirkungsgeschichte,"* in *Wahrheit und Methode* (Tübingen: J.C.B. Mohr, 1965), pp. 284–90.

16. Habermas very succinctly articulates Gadamer's position on language when he says that for Gadamer "the unity of language lost in the plurality of language games is dialectically restored in the context of tradition," *Zur Logik der Sozialwissenschaften* (Tübingen, 1967), p. 155.

17. *Phenomenology of Perception*, trans. Colin Smith (New York: Humanities Press, 1962), p. xix.

18. *Signs*, trans. Richard C. McCleary (Evanston: Northwestern University Press, 1964), p. 107.

19. John O'Neill, a social scientist who is at the same time a careful student of the thought of Merleau-Ponty, addresses this issue with insight when he writes: "Individual action, then, is the invention of history, because it is shaped in a present which previously was not just a void waiting to be determined by the word or deed, but a tissue of calling and response which is the life of no one and everyone. Every one of life's actions, in so far as it invokes its truth, lives in the expectation of an historical inscription, a judgement not of its intention or consequences but of its fecundity, which is the relevance of its 'story' to the present," *Sociology as a Skin Trade*, p. 233.

20. See the author's article, "The Historical as a Feature of Experience," *The University of Dayton Review*, Vol. 8, No. 1, 1971.

21. It is precisely this limitation that is discernible in the classical idealist philosophy of history, inaugurated by Hegel and continued in the reflections on history by such thinkers as R.G. Collingwood. When

Collingwood, for example, moves out from a consideration of historical consciousness to a definition of history as the "history of thought" we see the devaluation of the domain of praxis through the domination of idealist reflection. See particularly his work, *The Idea of History* (Oxford: Clarendon Press, 1946).

22. The phenomenon of forgotten language has been given some attention by Jacques Lacan in his structuralist reinterpretation of the unconscious. "The unconscious," he writes, "has nothing to do with instinct or primitive knowledge or preparation of thought in some underground. It is a thinking with words, with thoughts that escape your vigilance, your state of watchfulness," *The Languages of Criticism and the Sciences of Man: The Structuralist Controversy*, eds. R. Macksey and E. Donato (Baltimore: Johns Hopkins Press, 1970), p. 189. However, Lacan has difficulty avoiding a "linguisticism" of the unconscious because of his structuralist bias against the experiential and the historical as proper data for a science of man. Eugene T. Gendlin, who has also submitted a reinterpretation of the Freudian notion of the unconscious by relating it to the phenomenon of language, avoids the difficulty that we find in Lacan by restating the unconscious against the background of a dialectical interrelation of situations, language, and feelings. "To so restate the 'unconscious'," says Gendlin, "is to restate it in terms of a relationship between experience and explicatory statements," "Experiential Phenomenology," in *Phenomenology and the Social Sciences*, Vol. 1, ed. Maurice Natanson (Evanston: Northwestern University Press, 1973), p. 309. Gendlin's approach to the connection of language and the unconscious would thus appear to be more promising, principally because he is able to bring to this issue a carefully articulated notion of experience. See particularly his book, *Experiencing and the Creation of Meaning* (New York: Free Press, 1962).

23. Gerd Brand has argued that the rationality of myth provides the foundation for the objectivistic rationality of all science, including the natural sciences. See particularly his *Gesellschaft und persönliche Geschichte: Die mythologische Sinngebund sozialer Prozesse* (Stuttgart: Hohlhammer, 1972). We could quickly agree that certain mythic elements remain both in the concept formation and actual practice of the natural sciences, but we would resist the more general claim by Brand that the rationality of the natural sciences can ultimately be subsumed under the logos of myth. The blending of the logos of science with the logos of myth within the context of an expanded reason does not entail an absorption of the one by the other.

24. Albert Camus calls our attention to the abiding significance of mythic consciousness in his admirable short essay on "Prometheus in Hell" (*Prométhée aux enfers*): "Myths do not live by themselves. They wait for us to incarnate them. If a single man in the world responds to their call, they offer us their essence intact. We must preserve them and make sure that their sleep shall no longer be deadly, so that resurrection becomes possible," *Albert Camus,* ed. Germaine Bree (New York: Dell Publishing Co., 1963), p. 78.

25. See particularly his book, *Freud and Philosophy: An Essay on Interpretation,* trans. Denis Savage (Yale University Press, 1970).

26. *Phenomenology of Perception,* p. 290.

27. *Freud and Philosophy,* p. 35.

28. Foucault's archaeology of the human sciences culminates in a transformation of the representational prose of science and its world of things into a poeticized "being of language" and its anaclastic world of words. Allegedly having shown that the representative model of language has been dismantled in the discontinuous movement of *epistēmēs* throughout the history of the human sciences, Foucault then proclaims in a somewhat oracular fashion that we have now achieved that epistemological space that discloses the poetic archē of the sciences of man. The ultimate conclusion of Foucault's reflections on the origin of the human sciences is an inversion of positivism; the language of science itself is reduced to poetry. The thesis which we have maintained is not that science is to be displaced. The language and thought of science retain their integrity. The task is rather that of locating the origin of the human sciences in a prescientific and prephilosophical comprehension of the world, in which the mytho-poetic is indeed at work in the ongoing process of meaning-formation but not in such a manner that it negates the integrity of technical reason.

29. Cassirer, in this work, calls our attention to the recurring symbols of "Fortune" in the literature of political philosophy. He gives special attention to the Renaissance writings that deal with these symbols, and particularly the work of Machiavelli, who found it necessary to title one of his chapters in *The Prince,* "What Is Fortune and What Does It Mean?" This mythic element of Fortune, Cassirer demonstrates, continued to inform political thought up to the present day, receiving expression in various concepts of political destiny. (New York: Doubleday and Company, 1955).

INDEX

131